The Effects of Video Games on Children:
The Myth Unmasked

The Effects of Video Games on Children: The Myth Unmasked

Barrie Gunter

Sheffield Academic Press

302·2308
GUN

Published by Sheffield Academic Press Ltd
Mansion House
19 Kingfield Road,
Sheffield S11 9AS
England

Typeset by Carnegie Publishing, Chatsworth Rd, Lancaster
Printed on acid-free paper in Great Britain by
The Cromwell Press
Melksham, Wiltshire

British Library Cataloguing-in-Publication Data
A catalogue record for this book is available from the British Library

ISBN 1-85075-833-6

CONTENTS

PREFACE

Throughout the 1990s, increasing numbers of newspaper headlines have highlighted scare stories about violent and horrific video games, aimed at children and teenagers, with themes that emphasize murder and mayhem. Writing in *The Sunday Times* (5 October, 1997) Chris Dodd reported on the release into the UK market of *Postal*, the world's 'most violent video game'. According to Dodd, 'to win in the game players have to kill innocent bystanders, as well as armed opponents, before shooting themselves'. The title of the game is apparently based on the American phrase 'going postal' which was coined after a tragedy in 1986 when a postal worker shot dead 15 colleagues.

Another typical scare story which appeared in the *News of the World* (23 November, 1997), called for a ban on the 'criminal video game' *Grand Theft Auto* in which the player drives through busy city streets in stolen cars and is awarded points for shooting members of the public. In this case, a 'top policeman' was quoted arguing that this game could encourage young people to glorify such crimes and to become contemptuous of the law.

Invariably such stories include a call for tighter censorship of video games and assume as proven the conclusion that such games are invariably bad for children and teenagers who play them, primarily because they have the power to change young people's personalities and value systems for the worse.

Such concerns about the impact of new forms of media entertainment have a long history, which predates the appearance of computer games or, indeed, computers of any sort. They reflect similar public outcries which accompanied the growing popularity of early Hollywood movies in the 1920s and 1930s, horror comics in the 1950s, and television in the 1960s and later. The vehemence of concerns about video games stems not simply from the fact that some of them have violent themes, which makes them no different from other popular entertainment media such as movies and television, but perhaps more significantly from the fact that these games engage their players in a much more involving way than any other current media form. Video games are interactive. Game players do not just watch events happening on a screen in front of them, they are able to join in actively with those events and to some extent control what happens on screen. For some concerned lobbyists, this carries the young person into a different dimension of involvement from, say, ordinary television watching. The implications of this degree of cognitive and emotional engagement, to common-sense observers, are that there are bound to follow a series of profound and lasting adverse behavioural effects, changing the young people who play these games for the worse.

It is easy to criticize new forms of amusement, because they appear to involve people differently from older media, but what scientific evidence exists to support this view? Although, on the grounds of taste, everyone is entitled to voice their own opinion about whether they believe the content or theme of a video game should be deemed suitable material for children, or indeed for anyone, all too often criticisms of such games, together with calls for certain games to be banned, argue their case on the basis of assumed effects that playing such games can have on young people. Yet seldom do such critics present any conclusive scientific evidence to back up the accusations they level against video games.

This book represents an attempt to review research evidence on a series of different types of effect that have been associated with video games. Some of the effects are alleged to occur at a behavioural level, and more often than not place the spotlight on antisocial effects. Needless to say, some evidence has also emerged of healthier, prosocial effects deriving from video games. These effects may be behavioural, emotional or cognitive. Video games have been used in therapeutic contexts to deal effectively with emotional and behavioural problems among young people. Research has also surfaced to show that video games engage young people's minds in such a way that they may help to cultivate important new cognitive skills, which enable children and teenagers to process information more effectively than older generations can from multi-media presentations. It is therefore a myth that video games only do harm. It is equally a myth that all video games have the potential to do harm by virtue of their thematic content. Press reports would lead us to believe that practically all video games are violent.

This is untrue. There are many games which are wholly nonviolent in nature and which require players to use a range of cognitive abilities both to play the game and successfully to achieve the objectives that the game presents to them.

While we have already begun to learn a great deal about these games, the way they are played by and engage the attention of young people, and the social contexts in which they are played, there is still much more to learn. This book represents a start. In pulling together much of the existing research about video games, not only does it attempt to establish how much we currently know about the impact of playing these games, but, more significantly, how much we have yet to find out.

BG
November 1997

Chapter One

Video Games: What are the Concerns?

Early History

Playing games on computers can be traced back nearly 40 years, to a time when most computing was carried out on large mainframes. The introduction of minicomputers in the late 1950s opened up the possibility for individuals to interact with computers in a hands-on fashion. Computer programming could be undertaken at a keyboard rather than being reliant on punchcards. The earliest games were among the first programs created by undergraduate enthusiasts at the Massachusetts Institute of Technology. The first computer game, called *Spacewar*, a basic version of which later became the *Asteroids* arcade game, represented the outcome of these this early experimentation with programming (Laurel 1993; Levy 1984; Wilson 1992).

Other computer games followed as computers became more accessible to university researchers during the 1960s. Some of these games were computer versions of existing games, such as chess. Others were more original games purpose built for playing on computers, often with an adventure theme. These games were crude by today's standards, with players being required to type in commands to the computer to manipulate a character through various settings and problems. By the 1970s, computer games moved away from the confines of academic institutions into arcades where they became accessible to a much wider user group (Wilson 1992). By the early 1980s, computer game software production had become a major industry. By the 1990s, the leading games manufacturers were multi-billion dollar corporations associated with some of the best established and most widely known brand names of any product in the world.

As a form of computer-mediated play, commercial computer or video games represent a major entertainment phenomenon that has emerged over the past 20 years, bringing together computing, narrative structures and animated graphic art, and more recently realistic photographic or video forms (Kinder 1991). Video games represent a significant and dynamic step forward from traditional board games and even from television viewing. Video game play is interactive, whereas television viewing is physically passive (if you exclude zapping and zipping behaviour with remote control devices). Yet, compared with customary board games that require participants to create all the interaction, video games provide ready-made visual movement and sounds (Walker 1993). According to Real '... interactive games and entertainment lifted the potato off the couch and inserted the viewer into the action on the screen' (1996: 79).

The first electronic video games were introduced in the 1970s. In 1972, a coin-operated video game for arcades called *Pong*, manufactured in the United States by Atari, Inc., appeared on the electronic games market. *Pong* is an electronic ping-pong game for two players. The game was released in 1974 and sold more than 10000 units over the following year at more than $1000 each. Miday Manufacturing Co., which Atari licensed to produce a version of *Pong*, sold 9000 copies of the table-tennis-type game in less than six months.

The same year, a company called Magnavox marketed a video game called *Odyssey* that could be played on home television sets. The Odyssey set included a control unit that attached to a home television set and permitted a player to play 12 different games by inserting a "game card" into the control unit. The original Odyssey, however, was not a programmable video game. All 12 games were housed in the control unit and were not very different from each other.

In 1975, Atari entered the home video market with a version of *Pong* that offered several new advances: electronically generated on-screen courts; sound effects for every hit, miss and ricochet; and automatic on-screen digital scoring. By the end of 1976, 20 different companies were producing video games for home use in the United States. The same year Warner Communications acquired Atari and the following year introduced the first successful home video game package, the Atari Video Computer System.

In late 1976, Fairchild Camera and Instruments entered the field with the first fully programmable video system. The system was programmed by inserting an electronic cartridge into the game console. The benefit was that the player could play as many different games as the company provided cartridges. In 1977 and 1978, programmable video games for home use proliferated.

The first home computers were bought mostly by electronics hob-byists who had the skills necessary to build and maintain their own computer systems. Although the initial games offered relatively simple tasks and goals and a fairly restricted range of movements, they quickly became popular both in arcades and as home-based systems. In 1978, American shoppers spent more than $200 million on programmable home video games. By 1981, Americans were spending $5 billion on coin-operated games and another $1 billion on home television con-soles and cartridges. In 1982, electronic arcades in the United States that featured video games, took approximately $8 billion (US *News and World Reports*, 1982). At the same time, an additional $1.7 billion was spent on home video games (Alperowicz 1983).

During the 1983 to 1985 period, the video game market in the United States crashed as the market became saturated with poorly designed games. The early video and computer games, although compelling at the time, were one-dimensional, with fairly crude visuals. US sales plummetted from $2 billion in 1983 to $100 million in 1985. The industry was rescued by a 100-year-old Japanese playing card company called Nintendo, whose video games brought about significant advances in game sophistication, featuring a higher standard of graphics and versatility of movement on screen. These features characterized the Nintendo system launched in 1985 (Provenzo 1991). Other manufac-turers produced similarly advanced systems and games sales increased going into the 1990s. By the close of the 1980s, Nintendo controlled 80 per cent of the American video game market. During the 1990s, however, fierce competition arrived in the form of Sega.

Recovery of the video games market was also helped by the emergence of a new generation of children reaching game-playing age, whose growing computer literacy meant that these new, more sophisticated games, held special appeal (Leccese 1988; Salas 1988). By the end of the 1980s, video games dominated the entire toy market. In the United States 16 out of the 20 top-selling toys were video games (Playthings 1989).

Such was the value attached to new developments in video game products, that in Japan a new type of crime emerged involving the highway hijacking of new games. When the new Super Nintendo Enter-tainment System was released in Japan, the company created Operation Midnight to covertly distribute the product to retailers around the country, while keeping the release secret even from most Nintendo employees (Sheff 1993).

By 1994, Sega had moved ahead of Nintendo with the release of more advanced systems such as *Mortal Kombat*, characterized by much more graphically violent themes than earlier games. The market continued to grow and new games systems emerged from other manufacturers such as Panasonic, Philips and Pioneer, expanding the range of products available to ever-more discerning consumers (Shaffer 1993).

With the increased memory capacity offered by CD-ROM, the complexity of game configurations advanced considerably and contributed further towards their growing popularity. By 1994, however, the bubble appeared to have burst as sales of new cartridge games dropped. One reason for this decline in sales was uncertainty relating to the perceived long-term market prospects of recent and projected hardware innovations such as 'Expert Consoles' requiring a different level of computer literacy and games playing skill on the part of players (Buckman and Funk 1996).

Lately, however, the computer and video games market has shown signs of picking up once again, as a new generation of products has been introduced to the market. By 1995, a survey of television households across the United Kingdom revealed that more than 40 per cent of homes with children aged under 15 in them contained video games, more than double the percentage observed at the beginning of the decade (ITC 1996). Steiner (1996) reported that the computer games market was on the verge of a boom after two years of disappointing sales. Computer games manufacturers came under fire, however, for using advertising filled with horrific, violent imagery. One estimate put the worth of the computer and video games market in Britain alone at £600 million in 1996, an increase on the year before of nearly £100 million. This was still nearly £200 million down on three years earlier, illustrating the cyclical nature of this market. Sales figures tend to be sensitive to the launch of new games consoles every two years or so. One of the significant factors underlying games evolution is their increasingly large 'bit' sizes, starting at eight bits, and progressing to 16 and 32 bit machines. Future games are destined to attain 64 bits. Such increases in computing capacity will open up opportunities for yet more sophisticated games and configurations.

Popularity and Concern

With the introduction of more and more new games into the market and the advancements in game complexity and sophistication, computer and video games have attained widespread popularity in many western countries. As with any new medium of entertainment, however, particularly one so popular with children and teenagers, certain concerns have been voiced about undesirable physical, psychological and social side-effects of regular playing and, in some cases, an unhealthy level of pre-occupation with computer and video games. A 1984 Gallup poll indicated that more than 93 per cent of American teenagers had played video games for at least some of the time (*Athens Banner Herald* 1984). With this early popularity came a good deal of controversy. While video games clearly held a strong appeal for young people, who were predominant among players, not everyone thought they were a good thing. Across the United States, communities from Georgia to Massachusetts enacted local ordinances either banning arcades altogether or restricting access to them (*Newsweek* 1981).

A number of critics claimed that video games had a corrupting influence on the youth of the day. Video games were accused of glorifying violence and encouraging anti-social behaviour. Even the US Surgeon General at that time, C. Everett Koop, was quoted as saying that there was '... nothing constructive in the games ... Everything is eliminate, kill, destroy!' (Mayfield 1982). Politicians were joined by leading psychologists raising serious doubts about these games, such as Philip Zimbardo who observed that 'Eat him, burn him, zap him is the message, rather than bargaining and cooperation. Most games tend to feed into masculine fantasies of control, power and destruction' (Secunda 1983).

By the 1980s, researchers had begun to evaluate the impact of playing video games in many areas, including health, eye-hand coordination, patterns of daily activities, school performance, personality and psychopathology, and prosocial applications (see Funk 1993b; Funk and Buckman 1995). The value of studying play on both video and computer-based systems was recognized early (Greenfield 1984). Preliminary results presented at a conference sponsored by Atari in 1983 seemed to emphasize the positive aspects of game playing (*Video Games and Human Development* 1983). Research efforts decreased after this conference as sales declined in the early 1980s.

It is perhaps premature to conclude that playing electronic games is essentially a benign activity; video and computer games of the 1990s are more realistic and often more violent than their 1980s predecessors. As higher quality images and virtual reality technology enhance realism, game content must be evaluated from the participants' perspective.

Even in the early 1980s, reports emerged of an emotional backlash against the rising tide of popularity video games enjoyed among young people (Friedrich 1983). Several cities and towns in the United States were reported to have curtailed or banned public video game access (Favaro 1982). Although many communities engaged in raging debate over video games, little data existed at that time that clearly identified and substantiated the effects video games might have on children.

Video games as a cultural artifact have tremendous social importance because of their nature as a mass medium. For most children, video games are their introduction to the world of computer technology. Another factor, of course, is that they quickly became very popular and very pervasive among young people. A survey of high school students in California found that a clear majority reported playing games for about 1.25 hours a week in arcades and for nearly one hour a week at home (Rogers, Vale and Sood 1984).

Low cost microcomputers brought action-video games into many American households; a 1982 report showed that one in every ten households in the United States owned a home video game system (Perry, Truxal and Wallach 1982). A 1985-1986 survey in southern California found that 94 per cent of all ten-year-old children had played some video games (Rushbrook 1986). From December 1988, the Nintendo phenomenon brought video game sets into 14 million homes in the United States. As a further illustration of the diffusion of video games, in December 1991 there were more than 45 million Nintendo game sets in the United States, representing 34 per cent of all homes. In 1991, the home video game industry in the USA had $4.4 billion worth of sales. In 1992, Nintendo figures indicated that approximately 44 per cent of all US households had video game systems. The primary age range of Nintendo game players has tended to be six to 11 years, with 12- to 17-year-olds in second place (Berkhemer Kline Golin/Harris Communications, 1992). With this degree of market penetration, the video game has gone beyond a simple, one-to-one relationship with individual children to become part of child and adolescent culture in the United States and indeed around other parts of the world (Provenzo 1991).

Anxiety about the New Medium

The history of media developments is littered with examples of new forms of entertainment being introduced, attaining widespread popularity, and also attracting public concern because of their strong appeal to so many. Video games proved to be no exception to this rule. As their popularity grew rapidly so too did the level of public concern about the possibly deleterious impact of these games. For quite a number of years, however, there were few studies that attempted to explore the effects playing these games could have on young minds. Initially research concentrated on attempting to identify the social and personality correlates of playing video games (Dominick 1984; Gibb *et al.* 1983; Morlock, Yando and Nigolean 1985).

Anxieties about computer and video games can also be seen to reflect wider public concerns about the growing prevalence and increased use in various walks of life of information technology. From time to time, scare stories have surfaced in the press about the side-effects of using computers. These effects take on different forms in different countries. In Australia computer users have been found to fall foul of a condition called tenosynovitis (Ferguson 1987). In the United States, cataracts were thought to be caused by radiation emitted by VDU screens (Zarat 1984). The Scandinavians have reported facial rashes (Tjonn 1984), whilst elsewhere in Europe, there have been concerns about postural effects (see Loftus and Loftus 1983).

Any potential psychological effects are less tangible and therefore more disturbing than the more obvious accusations of physiological damage caused by excessive computer use. Anxieties and stress-related reactions towards working with new technology have already led to the coining of the term 'cyberphobia' (Weinberg 1971). This condition is described as exhibiting characteristics of rapid heart beat, nausea, diarhoea, and sweating.

Generalized fears seem to concentrate upon the belief that new technology strips people of their freedom and privacy. Thimbleby (1979) saw the potential for irreversible totalitarianism and oppression caused by the concentration of power in the hands of the few, and cites the example of police databases. Some observers have commented that computer professionals whose programs create such conditions are ill-equipped to perform their functions adequately. They are seen as lacking humanitarian concern, centring solely upon the capabilities of the computer rather than on the societal effects (Rothery 1971).

Computers have also been accused of causing such psychological and social effects as the deskilling of labour (Tuckman 1984), job stress, redundancy and unemployment, social isolation, and powerlessness (Mendelsohn 1983), and alienation (Sprandel 1982). Further, the use of computers has been charged with altering personalities (Weinberg 1971), with changing the socially gregarious into recluses and destroying relationships (Simons 1985). While many of these various concerns do not apply exclusively to computer and video games, they have, in many instances, been specifically associated at some time or another with an aspect of more entertainment-oriented computer-based products and applications.

— **Can Video Games become Addictive?**

One of the major concerns about video games is that they can become addictive (Anderson and Ford 1986). This issue is examined in more detail in Chapter Three. There has been some debate about whether it is appropriate or relevant to talk about 'addiction' in the context of computer or video game playing (Griffiths 1996). Addiction to video games may be like any other form of addictive behaviour. Players feel compelled constantly to be involved with these games and may display a lack of interest in other activities. If they try to stop playing for any length of time they experience withdrawal symptoms (Soper and Miller 1983). Elsewhere, excessive involvement with computer or video games has been discussed as a form of 'dependency' whereby playing with such games may not be a major preoccupation, but does serve particular social and psychological functions in players' lives in an especially pronounced fashion (Shotton 1989).

One further concern about video games, particularly if young people become addicted to playing them, is that they will cost them a lot of money. This might be a particular problem for those who play these games regularly in arcades. In Brooks's (1983) survey of young people of Southern California, eight out of ten respondents spent five dollars or less per week, the price of a movie. Only seven per cent spent the equivalent of their lunch money. In fact, because the regular players were also better players, they actually spent less money than less skilled adults would. In the world of video arcade games, skill is rewarded with play time, and a good player can play for an hour and a half for a single payment.

Indirect evidence of how desperate youngsters can become to play video games, once hooked on them, has derived from findings that some may resort to stealing money to play arcade games or to buy new games cartridges for home video games (Klein 1984; Keepers 1990; Griffiths and Hunt 1993). Others may go without food, by forfeiting their lunch money to pay for video games (McClure and Mears 1984) or play truant from school to play (Keepers 1990; Griffiths and Hunt 1993). Signs of withdrawal symptoms such as increased irritability when unable to play have also been found (Griffiths and Hunt 1993; Rutkowska and Carlton 1994).

The Problem of Violence

One of the principal concerns about video games and children has been that many of these games are characterized by themes of violence. As an extension of the wider public anxieties about the effects of media violence, concern in the context of video game influences has become focused around the fact that playing video games is interactive and therefore may be much more psychologically involving. In this respect, the impact of their violent themes upon young people could be more pronounced than that associated with mass entertainment media whose messages are passively received.

Some prominent psychologists in the United States have publicly expressed their concerns about the possible side-effects upon young-sters of playing with computer and video games with violent themes. Rogers (1982) was concerned that popular computer and video games with violent themes, particularly themes of nuclear conflict, constituted a trivialisation of the horror of war. Zimbardo (1982) felt that violence was too prominent a theme and that these games could be easily reprogrammed to include and promote cooperative and constructive behaviours. Loftus and Loftus (1983) noted that some games with positive themes were entering the market during the early 1980s. Popular games such as *Super Mario* featured a central character who exhibited selfless courage and determination to help others or rescue them from harm. Other games emerged during this period that had positive, helping themes, such as *Frogger* and *Donkey Kong*. In *Frogger*, the player is a frog whose objective is to cross a busy road, traverse a strip of land and a densely populated river. To achieve the end goal, the frog has to avoid the heavy traffic, running into snakes, being hit by logs and drowning in the river. Life is complicated by the appearance of a Lady Frog who the main Frog character marries and has to protect as well. *Donkey Kong* was a video game version of King Kong with the player having to save a young woman from the clutches of a big brown gorilla. While acknowledging the postive note struck by these games, Loftus and Loftus nevertheless had to concede that many of the most popular games available at that time did have predominantly violent themes. They were most concerned of all about games which involved killing people. They gave as one example the game *Death Race* in which the player controls a white car on the screen in which he or she relentlessly tries to run over little human beings who are trying to get out of the way. In another game called *Shark Attack*, four divers are pursued by a shark. The player controls the shark and the aim is to attack and kill the divers. Such games were regarded as having themes which were almost impossible to justify in any socially constructive sense (Loftus and Loftus 1983).

The possible effects of video violence are not easy to explain. While early evidence emerged that children who played with video games with violent themes such as *Space Invaders* and *Roadrunner*, displayed a rise in their level of aggressive play, other work indicated that video games could also have the opposite effect (Silvern, Williamson and Countermine 1983). It may be that the most harmful aspect of violent video games is that they are solitary in nature. A two-person aggressive game (e.g. video boxing) seems to provide a cathartic or releasing effect for aggression, while a solitary aggressive game (such as *Invaders*) may stimulate further aggression. More detailed evidence of the potential impact of violent computer and video games is discussed in Chapter Five.

One early observer of these games noted that the popularity of video games did not invariably seem to depend on how violent they were (Greenfield 1984). An important factor seemed to be how much action the game contained, rather than violence per se. Greenfield argued that manufacturers could afford to forsake violence for other forms of action, without risking a loss in popularity of their games. Indeed, some early evidence emerged that certain children might even be alienated from arcade games because of their violent themes. Malone (1981b) analyzed the appeal of *Darts*, a game designed to teach fractions to elementary school children. Introducing a fantasy aggression theme to this game enhanced its popularity among boys, but made it less popular with girls.

Is the Video Game Phenomenon Only Bad News?

Over the years, it has become increasingly recognized that children's education is not limited to formal schooling. There are many other ways in which children can learn factual knowledge and acquire a variety of cognitive skills (Greenfield and Childs 1991; Greenfield and Lave 1982; Guberman and Greenfield 1991; Rogoff and Lave 1984; Scribner 1986). The electronic media have become prominent sources of education, with the computer emerging most recently as the newest form of electronic medium. While serious computer packages have been developed with educational objectives, the most popular forms of computer activity fall within the context of entertainment. A fundamental question is whether computer games made primarily for entertainment purposes have any educational value.

One suggestion has been that there might be a set of literacy skills associated specifically with computers and video games that are distinct from the traditional literacy skills required for print media (Greenfield 1983, 1984, 1990). During the 1990s, studies have begun to emerge that have examined this issue directly. The early signs are that such skills may indeed exist and represent an important requisite in the effective playing of video games.

The Educational Promise of Video Games

Video games are a branch of computing. The microcomputer may be the most powerful yet of a long line of new technologies introduced throughout the present century, spanning television, radio and telecommunications (Lepper 1982). There is little doubt that since the beginning of the 1980s, the computer has brought about fundamental changes in industry, science and the workplace (Abelson 1982; Ginzberg

1982; Guiliano 1982). These computer-driven changes have also extended into education (Bracey 1982; Kulik 1982) and will cause a fundamental rethinking about the way education can and should be delivered in the future.

Proponents of video games have viewed them as a source of learning as well as entertainment. The kinds of activities involved in playing video games, it is argued by some, can promote eye-hand coordination or teach specific skills in spatial visualization or mathematics (Donchin 1983; Levin and Kareev 1981). Children engaged in such games may also acquire more generalized strategies for 'learning to learn' in novel environments (Stowbridge and Kugel 1983; Thornburg 1981, 1982). Mastery of such games is also viewed as a potential means of enhancing self-esteem among players who would otherwise be social misfits (Lynch 1983) and as a form of preparation for, or initiation into, the more cognitively demanding world of computer technology (Gabel 1983; Levin and Kareev 1981; Stowbridge and Kugel 1983).

There was some recognition that the skills required to play video games effectively could be applied to instructional applications of this medium (Malone 1981). As one writer observed, there was '... nothing mindless about mastering a video game' (Turkle 1984). These games demanded a great deal of skill and probably represented an essential early introduction of children to the computer culture.

Greenfield (1983, 1984) hypothesized that playing arcade-style action games could develop skills in inductive discovery, problem-solving through trial-and-error learning, and the ability to understand, manipulate and control visual events on screen. These games could also facilitate the transfer of skills to other tasks requiring the same sorts of cognitive skills. In an attempt to explain the psychology of video games, Loftus and Loftus (1983) proposed video games as potential training aids for people suffering perceptual disorders, for training eye-movement coordination, and for developing certain kinds of memory skills. The fact that video games do involve complex cognitive skills was demonstrated by Rabbit, Banerji and Szymonski (1989) who found that IQ, as measured by a standardized test, was highly predictive both of rate of learning and practised performance on an action video game.

The training potential of video games did not go unnoticed by the US military. Similarities were noted between the skills required to pilot an aircraft, for example, and those required to play video games (Nawrocki and Winner 1983). Both the US army and navy funded research on video games as training and performance testing tasks (Carter, Kennedy and Bittner 1980; Jones, Dunlap and Bilodeau 1986; Jones, Kennedy and Bittner 1981; Kennedy, Bittner and Jones 1981). These game simulators were used to train skills such as rapid information processing and the ability to think about a number of things at the same time (Trachtman 1981). This research established high correlations between performance on a flight simulator configured for aircraft carrier landing and performance on the Atari home video game *Air Combat Manoeuvring* (Lintern and Kennedy 1984). In this instance, the flight tasks involve keeping track of many different things and require a high level of skill in dividing attention between different events. This kind of cognitive ability is also required for the effective playing of certain video games.

The military have recognized other areas of relevance for video games, in recruitment and training (Provenzo 1991). The US Army modified the Atari game *Battlezone* for use in military training (Nawrocki and Winner 1983; Trachtman 1981). The US Navy designed its own video game, a war game called NAVTAG, intended for tactical training of junior officers (Jones 1984). Meanwhile, the British Navy has used a computer-based antisubmarine training game in a similar vein (Kiddoo 1982) and the US Army has established another game for a similar purpose (Compaine 1983).

One of the key points about video games is that players generally have to pick up the rules through trial-and-error and the testing of hypotheses rather than by being told in advance. This makes them, potentially, a powerful source of cognitive learning and skills acquisition. Players must figure out what different symbols and items on screen mean or represent and how they behave. In this way, video games encourage a style of thinking that resembles in many respects the kind of reasoning and deductions scientists have to make when investigating an issue for the first time (Greenfield 1983, 1984, 1993). If video games therefore train certain basic thought processes in this way, they could represent powerful training and learning tools. Chapter Four examines evidence for the potential cognitive skills benefits for children of playing video games in more detail.

Tracing the Appeal of Video Games

The growth of home computing has been described as a sociotechnical phenomenon, creating its own set of needs which in turn drive house-holders' demands for new commodities (Gershuny 1978, 1983). Video games are characterized by a variety of themes, and visual and sound features. These attributes combine to produce an electronic puzzle or task that the player must learn to master. A number of these features have been identified as having specific roles to play in generating the appeal that playing computer and video games seems to have for many young people. In some instances, the appeal of video games has been discussed in terms of textual analysis, while elsewhere the significance of specific game features has been investigated empirically.

A number of key features have been identified to underpin the appeal of computer and video games. Compared with standard board games or mechanical games, video games are in many ways more exciting, through their rapidly changing visual displays and offer more complex challenges to the skills of players (Provenzo 1991). The computational power of video games systems make it possible for scores to have virtually no upper limit, so that no matter how well a player performs, he or she can always attain a higher score (Turkle 1984). Video games intrinsically challenging and the main aim of playing is to become more skilful at playing the game itself. As Turkle noted, 'skill is the ultimate judge of competence' (1982: 37).

An essential feature of any computer or video game is that it must have an objective or goal. The goal may be to reach the end of a challenge, or simply to beat a previous best score. Supplementing this attribute are two others. First, there there must be a degree of challenge or difficulty. Not only that, there must be more than one level of difficulty. Unforeseen obstacles and problems must be put in the way of the player. The game's appeal can be further enhanced if it takes place in a fantasy context that involves the player in some emotional sense. Further, the game must offer some stimulation of the curiosity of the player, perhaps through its audio or visual effects, or through the different twists and turns of the game itself (Malone 1981a, b).

Rational analysis of the main attractions of Nintendo games, for example, have identified the inherent appeal to players as stemming primarily from their action and excitement, and the challenge posed to the player's own survival by various hazards and obstacles encountered at each stage in the game. Despite often borrowing themes from stories associated with other media (e.g. books, comics and movies), these games have tended to utilize these original themes more for their settings and characters than for their narratives. According to one observation:

> Nintendo^R's central feature is to construct presentation of spectacular spaces (or 'worlds', to use the game parlance). Its landscapes dwarf characters who serve, in turn, primarily as vehicles for players to move through these remarkable places. Once immersed in playing, we don't really care whether we rescue Princess Toadstool or not, all that matters is staying alive long enough to move between levels to see what spectacle awaits us on the next screen . . . Most of the criteria by which we might judge a classically constructed narrative fall by the wayside when we look at these games as storytelling systems. In Nintendo^R's narratives, characters play a minimal role, displaying traits that are largely capacities for action: fighting skills, modes of transportation, preestablished goals. The game's dependence on characters (Ninja Turtles, Bart Simpson, etc) borrowed from other media allows them to simply evoke those characters rather than to fully develop them. The character is little more than a cursor that mediates the player's relationship to the story world (Fuller and Jenkins 1995: 61).

Nintendo games have, then, been conceptualized as having ideological implications for users which derive from their use of significant historical events as the stages for action sequences. The spaces in which the game is played are often reconstructions of the sites of real events that may represent significant incidents in history. Thus, games that derive their stages from significant events in American history take children and the motives they already have as players to master the game and turn them 'into virtual colonists driven by a desire to master and control digital space' (Fuller and Jenkins 1995: 71).

Empirically-oriented studies have surveyed video game players for their opinions about specific games and investigated the significance of specific features in relation to players' involvement. Malone (1981b) analyzed the appeal of computer games, starting with a survey of the preferences of children who had become familiar with a wide variety of computer games in computer classes at a private elementary school in Palo Alto, California. The children ranged in age from about five to 13, and the games spanned the range from arcade games to simulations to adventure games to learning games. Visual elements were important in the games' popularity: graphics games such as *Petball* (computer pinball) and *Snake* 2 (two players controlling motion and shooting of snakes) were more popular than word games such as *Eliza* (conversation with a simulated psychiatrist) and *Gold* (a fill-in-the-blanks story about Goldilocks). A clue as to the attraction of moving visual images comes from the fact that the three most unpopular graphics games—*Stars*, *Snoopy* and *Draw*—had no animation at all or much less animation than more popular games.

According to Greenfield, if moving imagery is important in the popularity of video games, then perhaps the visual skills developed through watching television are the reason children of the television generation show so much talent with the games (Greenfield 1984: 89). Video games have the dynamic visual element of television, but they are also interactive. What happens on the screen is not entirely determined by the computer; it is also very much influenced by the player's actions. According to Greenfield

> It is possible that, before the advent of video games, a generation brought up on film and television was in a bind: the most active medium of expression, writing, lacked the quality of visual dynamism. Television had dynamism with an active participatory role for the child (1984: 90).

Malone (1981b) found that the presence of a goal was the single most important factor in determining the popularity of games. This is a quality that arcade games share with all true games. Other qualities he found to enhance the popularity of computer games were automatic scorekeeping, audio effects, randomness (the operation of chance), and the importance of speed (as in double solitaire) some of which are part of some conventional games. The others, automatic scorekeeping and audio effects, are essentially impossible without electronics.

When asked, players identify a number of specific features that characterize the games they like best. Myers (1990) used a Q-sort methodology in which video game players sorted a set of statements about video games into groups that represented particular attributes. Four aesthetic criteria of an appealing video game emerged. Games must offer a challenge through creating situations where there is a degree of uncertainty about the outcome. They should evoke the player's curiosity. They should have a fantasy element that involves the player in an escapist manner. Finally, games should be fully interactive and react quickly to the player's moves.

The Challenge of Video Games

Children look for video games that offer an intellectual challenge. Most games have varying levels of difficulty and children look to master one level and move off to a more challenging level. Evidence from work with learning-disabled children in an after-school educational setting emphasized the appeal of levels of increasing difficulty. Greenfield (1984) reported on one such case where, once children had mastered all levels of difficulty in a particular game, they stopped playing it.

Arcade games have been found to be better educational tools for learning-disabled children than 'educational' games or education in general. Children who avoided instruction during reading time were willing to be instructed during computer time. Some children who refused to concentrate on conventional learning tasks concentrated very well on arcade-style games, showing perseverance and making a great deal of progress from trial to trial. In Chapter Six, research on the positive and negative health implications associated with playing video games is examined. From this evidence, while there have been some signs that excessive playing of these games can give rise to physical ailments and, among the predisposed, may cause epileptic seizures, equally there are indications that video games can be used in a beneficial, therapeutic way to treat children with behavioural problems.

During the 20-year history of video games, attention was initially focused on the potential harms that these games could cause among young players. The main concerns rested on the observations that children could apparently become hooked on playing video games and would do so to excess and to the consequent neglect of other activities. Not only did the games preoccupy their time, they also frequently exposed youngsters to and involved them actively in antisocial and violent themes giving rise to worries about unwanted behavioural effects. It was suggested that video games represented a new form of addictive behaviour among children and teenagers that could have undesirable physical, mental, social and economic side effects.

By the mid-1980s, however, the thinking and the work of scholars such as Patricia Greenfield in California, the geographical source of so many developments in computing, began to shift the focus towards a realization that video games could have cognitive and behavioural benefits for children. In a world increasingly dominated and run by computers, playing video games served as an introduction to computing, which provided an opportunity for youngsters to develop and practise the cognitive skills needed to operate computer technologies effectively. Research evidence began to emerge that far from impeding intellectual growth, computer and video games invoked and stimulated certain categories of mental abilities, especially those concerned with the effective processing of information presented in images. Regular playing of video games developed a quickness of thought in situations where individuals were required to act upon parallel streams of informational input, and where any hesitation resulted in the player being overwhelmed by the game.

Despite their popularity, the research literature on video games remains fairly limited, having only just begun to scratch the surface of understanding about how children and teenagers use them and the effects they might have upon those young people who play them on a regular basis. As with most media research, the focus of empirical enquiry has tended to become pinned to a relatively narrow range of content categories and types of impact. It is perhaps understandable, given the history of mass media research and of public concerns about media effects, that initial enquiries should be drawn to investigate the potential impact of video games with violent themes. Yet these themes are not the only ones to be found, and are by no means overwhelmingly dominant either in terms of what types of games exist or in terms of which games are the most popular. The aim of this book is to provide an up-to-date review of what has been found out about the way video games are played and the role they occupy in the lives of young people, and about the effects—good or bad—they may have upon those who play them.

Chapter Two

Tapping Into
Players' Habits and Preferences

Video game playing has become a widespread and popular pastime among millions of children and teenagers. While much of the early focus of research into their impact on young people centred on arcade video games, these games today can be enjoyed via other hardware systems including hand-held games, personal computers and home video consoles. The debate about video games has tended to be concerned most of all with the alleged harms the over-playing of such games can have upon children and teenagers, which is believed to affect their intellectual development and social behaviour.

It was noted in Chapter One, for instance, that both national and local legislators and policy makers in some countries have had negative reactions to children's and teenagers' video game playing, whether it takes place in or out of the home. The US Surgeon General, C. Everett Koop, warned about what he believed to be the addictive nature of video games, which could increase violent behaviour in children. As a reaction to this adverse publicity, many local and state governments in the United States, placed bans on or regulated the use of video games (Mitchell 1985). These reactions were further fuelled by research findings that emerged at about the same time, suggesting that video game playing was associated with falling school grades, feelings of guilt and the excessive spending of money (Soper and Miller 1983).

Before turning to the evidence on the good or bad effects of playing video games, in this chapter attention is focused upon patterns of usage and game preferences. To what extent and in what ways do children and teenagers use video games? What do they like or dislike about these games? How does the use of video games fit in with other activities in young people's lives? These are some of the questions that will be addressed in this chapter. The extent of video game playing and preferences for particular kinds of games may also be linked to inherent characteristics of the players. Research has shown that demographic factors and personality factors are associated with differential use of video games. The current chapter will examine how patterns of video game usage and attitudes towards these games may vary between different types of young people.

The Uses and Roles of Video Games

Many early efforts to understand video games were subsumed under research into the reasons why people acquired home computers. Initial investigations of the home computer phenomenon deployed a variety of research methodologies to investigate factors linked to initial acquisition of personal computers and related software, in an attempt to find out what attributes characterized early adopters (Danko and Maclachlan 1983; Dickerson and Gentry 1983; Hall, Nightingdale and MacAuley 1985). This work revealed little about the reasons why some people were willing and able to acquire these machines, however (Murdock, Hartmann and Gray 1992). Home computers were often marketed as having important educational benefits for users, while at the same time providing a source of novel entertainment. Home computer acquisition also depended, though, on consumers having the necessary resources to purchase the basic machine and the various accessories that went with it and made it operational.

Rogers and Larsen (1984) studied patterns of adoption and use of personal computers and focused on how far the personal needs and dispositions of users were met by the machines available at the time. These authors asked users what they wanted a personal computer for, whether they had any relevant skills or experience, and whether they had been pleased or disappointed with the equipment they had acquired. Less attention was given to economic considerations that were found by others to have an important bearing on personal computer uptake (Murdock, Hartmann and Gray 1992). While a consumer might be able to afford the basic personal computer, for some machines extra payments were necessary for a dedicated monitor, printer and software. Models that combined these elements for an affordable price tended to be among the most popular as the market was becoming established.

In Britain, early successes included Sinclair and Commodore machines, which were used primarily for their game-playing potential. They had a relatively low price and did not need a disk drive or dedicated monitor. They could be operated through a standard black-and-white television set and software could be stored on a portable audio-cassette recorder. These selling points also imposed their own constraints in that they were slow to prepare and use, and offered systems that were not particularly robust. The novelty value of such items meant that their relative clumsiness did not matter, but they were clearly destined to be overtaken in due course by more powerful and advanced micro-computer technology.

Within the wider context of home computing, computer or video games have represented a form of recreational pursuit and for regular players these games become an integral part of their leisure activities. When questioned about their use of computers, American high school students in the mid-1980s indicated a variety of different applications within the school context (e.g. unspecified programming work, use of graphics packages, learning how to program, word processing, doing class projects and other classwork, and also playing games and programming their own games), but a narrower range of applications in the home context, where computer use was dominated by playing video games and unspecified programming (Braun *et al.* 1986).

Concerns have been expressed that video games are addictive for youngsters and implicit in this concern is a belief that these games are inherently harmful to young people (Greenburg 1981; Mandel 1983). As an addiction that costs money, if young people become hooked on playing these games there is the accompanying worry that they will spend inordinate amounts of time and money on playing. As well as putting a financial strain on young pockets, video game addiction is thought to displace other leisure activities that may be healthier, produce poorer performances at school because of a lack of effort in doing homework and tiredness, and provide less opportunity for youngsters to develop social skills because of the belief that playing video games is a basically lonely pursuit.

These ideas about video game playing, however, have not been consistently supported through research. Surveys of young people's attitudes towards video games and observational studies that have monitored video arcade behaviour have often failed to corroborate the impression given by critics of these games that youngsters become addicted and that their school work and social lives deteriorate as a direct result. In the early 1980s, when video games were first becoming established, one survey of American adolescents and young people, aged from ten to 20 years, found little support for the notion that playing these games reduced participation in active sports or that it was related to poor school performance. With few exceptions, playing video games was a minor part of young people's lives and was generally held in perspective with other leisure activities. Those young people who played these games were rated as somewhat above average at school. Some evidence emerged also that adolescents who played video games exhibited greater interest in learning about computers (Egli and Meyers 1984).

For some of the young people in this American survey, video game playing did show elements of being a compulsive behaviour. These people played the most and indicated that they felt somewhat addicted to playing video games, tended to enjoy video game playing more than almost anything else, and were more inclined to be competitive. When asked, several of those who answered strongly that they felt addicted explained their responses by saying they felt a strong impulse to play the games whenever they were around them. Placed in an environment with video games present, playing was difficult to resist. Individuals who exhibited any compulsive tendencies represented a minority group, comprising around ten per cent of those who were interviewed.

With young children, some researchers have made comparisons between those youngsters who have just obtained a video game for the first time and those who have had longer experience of owning and playing video games. Creasey and Myers (1986) compared three groups of children aged between nine and 16 years over a five-month spell. These included a new game group, who received a home video game system in December; an old game group who had owned a video game system for a year; and a no-game group who did not own a video game system. The children responded to questionnaires about their leisure activities, their school work, and their relationships with friends and peers at two points in time, first in November and then again in March, some three months after new game users had received their first video game. The new game children were also interviewed briefly in January, just three weeks after they had got their video game.

Children with a new video game system spent a great deal of time playing with it, at least at first. This involvement rapidly dropped off. The new game group spent an average of over 15 hours a week (or more than two hours a day) playing video games during their first three weeks of owning a game, but after three months this amount of playing time had reduced by half. Children who had had a video game for a year or more showed even lower levels of playing, averaging just over two hours a week with video games.

The extent to which children play video games may have something to do with the kinds of gratifications they get from this activity. Certainly, a novelty factor may be in operation initially, but in the longer term, the continuing appeal of video games is likely to be dependent upon their ability to entertain or challenge youngsters in a way other activities cannot. Several studies have revealed an important social gratification component to video game playing, especially where it takes place in video arcades. The evidence here, however, has not always been consistent

One observational study of young people playing video games in arcades in Los Angeles found that players spent less than half their time in the arcade actually playing the machines, while much of the remainder of their time was spent engaged in other activities with friends (Brooks 1983). Other observers have found, however, that much video game playing in arcades was itself a solitary activity, with only around 40 per cent of players surveyed accompanied while playing by one or more other people (Braun *et al.* 1986).

In a survey of American children aged between ten and 14 years, Selnow (1984) reported that video game playing among this age group was linked to specific gratifications that the games satisfied for these young people. Key to the continuing appeal of video games were the perceptions that: (1) they were found to be more fun than human companionship; (2) they could teach things about other people and how to behave around others; (3) they offered companionship in a way similar to being with a friend and could help some children forget about being alone; (4) they allowed the player to have a direct, personal involvement in the action of the game; and (5) they could also provide a means of escape from life's problems.

Clearly, these perceptions embrace a variety of gratifications and it is not the case that all video game playing children would identify strongly with every one of these needs that games would appear to have the capacity to satisfy. Nevertheless, Selnow's study revealed that children who were the more frequent video game players identified with and endorsed more of these gratifications than did relatively infrequent players. The finding that active involvement with the action of the video game was an important factor underlying their appeal was a feature which set playing video games apart from viewing television. While watching television was found to satisfy the other four gratifications to the same degree as video games, the interactivity-related gratification set playing these games apart.

Children who spent more time and money on video games were also more likely to agree that playing the games was more fun, more exciting and generally more desirable than being with human companions. Video games were also seen as offering an opportunity to learn about other people. The reason for this could be that video game players recognize that arcades are places where their peers congregate. This provides them with opportunities to observe others and to learn how they behave, as well as learning how to behave around other people. This function is served not by the games themselves but by the social environment that video game arcades represent. At the same time, the interaction between player and video game could be so engaging that the games themselves come to be seen as surrogate companions.

In Britain, interviews with adolescents in amusement arcades have revealed that these locations represent meeting places and somewhere to go to spend time. It is recognized by those who go to them that arcades are places where you can not only meet existing friends but also make new friends and hang out with the social crowd. Many arcades had the added attractions of providing a warm, friendly and relaxed atmosphere, and affording free entry. For some individuals, however, regular visits to arcades were motivated by a strong need to play the machines. Some of these players were driven by the need to develop a sense of mastery and control over the machines. For others, playing games machines provided a means of escape from outside reality, an opportunity to forget about one's problems, and a distraction to relieve depression (Griffiths 1995).

Evidence emerged, again in Britain, that computer or video games represented a new sub-cultural phenomenon among young people. For boys, in particular, computer games were a source of conversation. This was often displayed as rivalry over specific models, and the offering of expert advice on the best games to get and the most effective strategies of play, as well as boasting about past successes in the scores allegedly obtained on different games (Haddon 1992). Conversations would include evaluation of hardware and software, the next purchases to which they aspired, the costs of products and where to buy them. As Haddon observed following a study of children's use of home computers:

> Games talk could ... be competitive, emphasizing superior skills in terms of the scores which had been achieved, the relative size of the boys' game collections, and who possessed the latest games ... newsworthy talk also covered items such as which games had recently been released and were in vogue, what features they possessed, and what might be in the pipeline from the arcades or as a conversion from another machine format (1992: 88).

Girls exhibited much less personal computer-related talk than did boys but were still mainly interested in computers from the games playing perspective. In general, girls did not talk about computers much at all, were not avid readers of computer magazines as were boys, and usually relied on brothers or male peers for information about games. Gender differences in computer game involvement are discussed in more detail later in this chapter.

Parental Views

Parents as well as politicians have expressed concerns about the potential impact of video games on children. The opinions held by parents, however, very often differ from those held by children and are sometimes contrary to the findings of formal research into the impact of these games. A survey of public opinion towards new media technologies in Britain found that adult respondents believed video games could be disruptive to family life (Breakwell *et al.* 1986).

In the United States, a survey of media scholars asked for their opinions about their own children's involvement with television. Interesting differences emerged between the views expressed by these experts and the findings of published research. The biggest difference concerned perceptions of the contribution of television to children's aggressive behaviour. The researchers reported that '... 44 per cent of the sample asserted that TV was only a somewhat important cause of youth violence, and 24 per cent of the sample insisted that no relationship exists between TV and children's aggressive behaviour' (Bybee, Robinson and Turow 1985: 150).

A further study revealed that parents and their children often disagree about the impact of mass media on children themselves. Sneed and Runco (1992) invited groups of parents and their children separately to list the kinds of effects television and video games can have on children. Parents' opinions were also compared with those given by a sample of adults without children. Both groups of adults—parents and non-parents—held similar beliefs about the influence of television, but differed in their views about video games, with parents generally holding more positive impressions about video games. Children held more positive beliefs about the influence of television than their parents, but both parents and children held similar beliefs about the influence of video games. In particular, children were less likely to believe in the alleged negative influences of television than were parents and were more likely to believe that it could have positive influences. Children were also less likely to believe that television influenced how much time they spent on other activities. In fact, children were more likely to believe that television was associated with increased originality of thought and better problem-solving abilities.

While it is understandable that parents may worry that owning a home video game will hurt their child's study habits and school performance, this fear was not supported, for instance, by research conducted by Creasey and Myers (1986). In this study, even initial ownership of a video game appeared to make little or no difference to a child's home-work time or school grades in mathematics or English. The only difference to emerge at all was the finding that children whose parents had not bought them a video game, had higher maths grades. This result cannot be causally attributed to the playing of video games, however. Instead, it is more likely that children with higher grades in mathematics had parents who were less inclined to buy them a video game system.

Research in Britain has found that some parents do report trying to exercise control over their children's playing with personal computers. This is not always easy, however, especially where it concerns older teenagers who may be significantly more competent in computer usage than their parents (Murdock, Hartmann and Gray 1992).

Who Plays Video Games?

Video games are played by people of all age groups (Surrey 1982). The market is dominated, however, by young males in their teens or early twenties. By the early 1980s, surveys showed that around nine out of ten teenagers in the United States played video games (Atari 1982; Gallup 1982). As the popularity of video games became firmly established in the 1980s, surveys of computer and video game players revealed that playing time could range from two hours a week to two hours a day (Funk 1993a). The amount of time devoted to computer or video games depended to some extent on how long individuals had been playing. Some research indicated that initial daily play might occur for two hours or more a day, but then drop off to about a couple of hours a week after just a few months (Creasey and Myers 1986).

⇁ Gender Differences

Video games have greater appeal to some groups than to others. One of the key discriminating factors among children and adolescents in the playing of video games is gender. Gender differences have been observed in patterns of computer and video game play. Boys generally play more often than girls both at home and in amusement arcades (Dominick 1984; Griffiths 1991b; Kubey and Larson 1990). Observations of video arcade game players under natural circumstances have shown, from early on in the history of study of video games, that males played to a greater extent than females during the morning on the way to work, during their lunch break and again in the evening after work (Trinkaus 1983). Loftus and Loftus reported a survey of video game playing conducted in Minneapolis: 'After surveying 2,000 video game players in several age groups, it was concluded that heavy players (those who played at least once a week) were mostly teenage males' (1983: 106). A survey of video arcade traffic in a suburban Pittsburgh shopping mall revealed that most players were boys. Few girls were observed to play the games by themselves. In fact, most of the girls were with boys and mostly watched them play (Kiesler, Sproull and Eccles 1983). Another video arcade study surveyed the video game playing pursuits of nine- to 15-year-old boys and girls. The children who went to arcades were found to score lower in terms of masculinity and femininity on a sex-role inventory, which suggested that video game players had less well-defined sex-role preferences than did children who never went to video game arcades (Melancon and Thompson 1985).

A survey of video game playing among ten- to 12-year-olds in the San Francisco Bay area found that boys played video games more often both in arcades and in the home (Linn and Lepper 1987). In another survey of 16- and 17-year-olds in three high schools in Georgia, Dominick (1984) reported that the average playing time per week was one and a half hours for boys compared to less than one hour for girls. A similar relationship between gender and frequency of video game playing was subsequently found among college students (Morlock, Yando and Nigolean 1985). In an observational study of traffic flow through several sites, video arcades were found to be basically male preserves (Kiesler, Sproull and Eccles 1985). Explanations of this phenomenon were that females may feel less comfortable than males with the violent themes that are found in many video games, and less comfortable in the arcade atmosphere where such games are played (Kiesler, Sproull and Eccles 1983). Girls generally seem to show a much lower level of interest in video games than do boys (Greenfield, Camaioni *et al.* 1994; Subrahmanyam and Greenfield 1994). Why do such differences occur?

As home systems have become so widely available, this now tends to be where most game playing takes place (Funk 1993a; Kubey and Larson 1990). Here, as in arcades, the most frequent players have tended to be teenage males (Loftus and Loftus 1983). While video game playing has been most widespread in the United States, where most of the research into its use and impact has also been carried out, the predominance of young male players has been the typical pattern in other countries as well (Griffiths 1991b). Research with 11- to 16-year-olds in Britain found that over three out of four (77 per cent) claimed to play video games (Phillips *et al.* 1995). The most common pattern was to play each day, on average for around 30 to 60 minutes. A small proportion of players (7.5 per cent) was identified whose behaviour was more extreme than this in that they reported much greater than average amounts of video game play and felt that it had caused them to neglect other activities such as homework. In general, males claimed to play with computer games more than girls, and were more likely to report playing to the neglect of homework. Another British survey with a similarly aged sample of children and teenagers confirmed that boys played with computer games more than did girls, even though both sexes displayed equal interest in playing (Colwell, Grady and Rhaiti 1995)

Gender differences in computer use were consistently reported in Britain in the mid-1980s in family households that had acquired home computers. In these homes, the main user tended to be male (e.g., Wheelock 1992). The main user was female in just one in seven cases. Among the teenage children surveyed in these households, boys were twice as likely as girls to play with computers once or twice a week, and were six times as likely to play three or more times a week (Murdock, Hartmann and Gray 1992).

A number of reasons have been forthcoming about why males and females differ in their frequency of video game playing. One explanation has linked this gender difference to the content of many games. The gender biased pattern of computer or video game playing was contributed towards from early on by the distinct gender bias in game themes. Most early arcade games, for example, comprised either simulations of male activities such as flying a fighter aircraft or driving a racing car, or consisted of situations in which a player defended territory against enemy attack. The most famous example of this last kind was *Invaders*, launched in 1979. Another observation was that video games rarely featured female characters. One American analysis found that, by the mid-1980s, women appeared in only eight per cent of arcade games, and then occupied mainly passive roles (Toles 1985).

According to one author, video games are produced by males for males (Gutman 1982). Some analyses of the themes of video games have found that games are more likely to contain masculine images than feminine images (Braun *et al.* 1986). In most games, for example, the player controls a male character (Provenzo 1991; Rushbrook 1986) who is carrying out activities that are perceived to be male oriented (Hess and Miura 1985). Another factor may be the way males and females are socialized. Women are more conditioned than men to suppress the expression of aggression in public and may therefore feel less comfortable playing games of combat or war (Surrey 1982). In a study of undergraduate video game players, males reported that they played to master the games and for competition whereas females preferred more whimsical, less aggressive and less demanding games (Morlock, Yando and Nigolean 1985). Recent British research has indicated that girls may exhibit as much interest in computers and associated games as do boys, but boys spend more time playing computer and video games. Heavy players among boys are also often likely to say they prefer playing computer and video games to seeing their friends. Despite this, those same individuals nevertheless see their friends often outside school, thus contradicting the view that computer games take the place of normal social contact (Colwell, Grady and Rhaita 1995).

Research in the Netherlands has provided further support for the idea that boys prefer aggressive themes more than girls. Children's preferences for video games with violent themes was measured by asking them to write down their five most liked and frequently played video games. The games named were subsequently scored for their violence content by a panel of video game experts. Results showed that boys spent more time playing video games than girls. Boys also showed a stronger preference for playing video games with violent themes. In explaining why boys spent more time on video games and their preference for violent games, the researchers adopted Eagly's (1987) social role theory. Themes of video games often revolve around competition and most video games contain acts of violence. Thus, a great deal of the video games answer to the masculine gender stereotype (Schie and Wiegman 1996).

In view of the male bias in video game design and video game play, a number of writers have expressed the concern that females might be at a disadvantage where computer usage is concerned, because computer and video games might provide an easy lead-in to computer literacy (Lepper 1982; Loftus and Loftus 1983; Greenfield 1984).

Whatever the precise nature of the content of video games, there is evidence that males have more intense experiences than do females when playing video games. In one study, college students gave researchers a series of verbal reports regarding their emotional states while playing video games. They were asked, in particular, if they experienced such emotions as anger, frustration, excitement, sexual arousal and joy or exhilaration when playing. While sexual arousal turned out to be irrelevant in this context, on all the other emotional reactions male college students generally reported more intense experiences while playing video games than did their female counterparts. Women's emotional reactions exceeded those of men, however, in terms of excitement and intensity of frustration, possibly the latter response being linked to their generally lesser competence at playing these games (Kaplan and Kaplan 1981).

A further factor that may explain differences between males and females in their video game playing preferences is the psychological fact that males generally perform better than females in terms of their visual and spatial skills (Maccoby and Jacklin 1974). These skills are essential in good game playing since good eye-hand coordination is needed in addition to the quick judgments of spatial relationships (Kiesler, Sproull and Eccles 1983). Given that girls often scored lower than boys on video games because they lacked certain essential skills, could have further discouraged them from wanting to play.

The gender difference in key cognitive skills linked to video game playing has been supported by research conducted across cultures. Male university students in Rome and Los Angeles were found to show more skill on the average video game, both initially and after several hours of practice, than did female university students. Both genders exhibited similar rates of skill improvement however (Greenfield, Camaioni *et al.* 1994).

In a further study, female players were recruited without advance knowledge that the study involved video games (Greenfield, Brannon and Lohr 1994). In addition, the experimental task was to learn a violent action game—*The Empire Strikes Back*. In that study, male players generally mastered the game whereas the female players did not, even though they played more games in their attempts to reach a certain standard.

It seemed quite possible that the problem of female mastery in this research might have arisen from the violence in the particular game that was used. Research on video game tastes indicates that whereas boys are turned on by a violent game theme, girls are turned off (Malone 1981). Studies of children and adult television preferences confirm this finding. Boys and men are much more attracted to violent action themes than are girls and women (Condry 1989). With this in mind, a further study was designed to explore gender issues using a nonviolent action game, *Marble Madness* (Subrahmanyam and Greenfield 1994). In that study, eleven-year-old boys and girls were not significantly different in video game skill at the outset of game play. After a few hours of practice, however, the average boy performed better in the game than did the average girl.

However, action per se is recognized by children as a male characteristic, according to research on responses to television commercials with different formal features (Welch *et al.* 1979). Hence, the genre of action video game could by its very nature have greater appeal for boys than for girls. Contrary to this explanation, Subrahmanyam and Green-field (1994) informally observed that children of both genders preferred the action game *Marble Madness* to the control condition, a non-action computer word game called *Conjecture.* For whatever reason, however, it is clear that males do have more video game experience than females, both in childhood (Subrahmanyam and Greenfield 1994) and adulthood (Greenfield, Brannon & Lohr 1994; Greenfield, Camaioni *et al.* 1994). Through this experience, they may have 'learned how to learn' to play video games, therefore benefiting more from video game practice. Myers's (1984) extensive ethnographic study in a computer store con-firmed the development of such learning strategies.

Another factor in better average male performance on video games could be that the average male may take a more experimental (trial and error) approach to the games than the average female. That is, the average male may be more willing than the average female to learn by acting before he understands all of the rules of the game. Smith and Stander (1981) found this to be the case with anthropology students who were first-time users of a computer system. This gender difference in being willing to act without full understanding could be related to the possible link between male gender and physical action. Given an interactive medium in which experimentation yields instant feedback, an experimental approach logically has to be of great advantage.

Gender differences in the application of logical and strategic planning skills to game playing may also be a factor in gender differences in learning to play video games. Mandinach and Corno (1985) found that boys used these processes more than girls and were more successful at playing a computer adventure game called *Hunt the Wumpus.* These differences showed up despite equal experience with computers in general and equal liking for the game.

Buckman and Funk (1996) reported a survey of 900 American children from grades four (age ten) to eight (age 14), fairly evenly divided among girls and boys. The children indicated how much time they devoted in a typical week to playing computer and video games at home or in an arcade. The amount of home-based game playing declined steadily with age. About 90 per cent of fourth graders reported playing one or more hours per week at home compared to about 75 per cent of seventh and eighth graders. Some weekly arcade play was reported by about 50 per cent of fourth graders and by around 75 per cent of eighth graders. Playing more than ten hours a week at home was reported by 22 per cent of fourth graders and five per cent of eighth graders. Fewer still in each case reported this amount of weekly arcade attendance (4 per cent).

Boys reported significantly more electronic game playing than girls across all age groups, both in respect of at-home and arcade play. Fourth grade girls reported about five and half hours a week of game playing, while by eighth grade this had dropped to an average of two and a half hours. For boys, the playing times for these age groups averaged nine and a half hours and five hours per week respectively.

In the same survey, video game preferences were measured by asking the children to list the titles of up to three favourite games. These were then classified by the researchers into General Entertainment, Educational, Fantasy (Cartoon) Violence, Human Violence, Sports, and Sports Violence. An independent panel of youngsters aged eight through 17 described the primary action and goal of each listed video game title, enabling the researchers to assign each title to the appropriate thematic category.

Both gender and age distinguished game theme preferences. Educational games became less popular and General Entertainment games became more frequently preferred with increased age, among both boys and girls. Fantasy and Human Violence themes were the most popular of all themes across all age groups, with boys being more likely to prefer Human Violence and girls more likely to opt for Fantasy Violence. Sports games were better liked by boys, while younger girls were more likely than older girls to name titles from this category among their favourites. Sports Violence preferences were surveyed only among grades four to six, where boys exhibited a greater preference for such games than did girls.

Personality Differences

Some researchers have looked beyond gender and explored the possibility that differences in frequency of video game playing as well as preferences for particular types of video games might be explained by personality factors. The results, so far, have been mixed. Some indications have emerged that gender differences in video game playing could be linked to personality variables, but personality measures have not consistently exhibited significant relationships with game playing behaviour or content preferences.

Before research attention was directed at entertainment-oriented video games, research in the early 1970s revealed that computer programmers tended to be introverted, youthful, single males (Barnes 1974). Such individuals were also found to have strong interests in mechanical activities, but were less skilled in social situations (Cross 1972). High abstract reasoning skills were found to be a primary factor differentiating successful from unsuccessful programmers (Miller 1970). Although these studies were not carried out with video game players, they nevertheless opened up the possibility that involvement with computer-related activities might be linked to personality characteristics.

Gibb and his colleagues examined personality differences among high and low electronic video game users during the early 1980s in the United States. Male and female players were compared on a number of personality measures including self-esteem–self-degradation; social deviancy–social conformity; hostility–kindness; social withdrawal–gregariousness; obsession–compulsion; and achievement motivation. There were no major differences between males and females in terms of personality profiles, nor did any personality measures exhibit any significant overall degree of association with frequency of video game playing. However, one interesting finding to emerge was that females with longer playing experience tended also to be more achievement motivated than members of their own sex with less playing experience (Gibb *et al.* 1983).

One explanation for this was that the video games themselves were likely to hold greater appeal for achievement-oriented individuals because they invited players to constantly improve on their previous scores and to achieve higher and higher levels of performance. Those females with strong achievement motivation could be expected to find the games attractive because they invited players to attain higher levels of achievement on which they received immediate feedback. Females who scored higher in terms of obsessive-compulsive characteristics tended to find video games less appealing because better performance often required an adaptive and flexible pattern of responding rather than mastery of a rigid response pattern.

A subsequent survey of video game playing attitudes among American high school teenagers provided corroboration for some of the earlier results. Once again, males were found to play video games more often than did females. Frequent video game players, however, also liked competitive activities, such as playing sports. Such individuals welcomed challenges and situations in which they were required to achieve higher levels of competence. Infrequent players not only tended to be female, but also eschewed competitive activities more generally. These infrequent players did not like video games, were anxious about computers and also read fewer books. Indeed, the brighter the teenagers, the more likely they were to feel comfortable with computers. Brighter teenagers did not play more often, but they did differ from the less bright in the way they played. Brighter youngsters tended to prefer playing adventure and simulation games to arcade games (McClure and Mears 1984).

Not all researchers have found personality differences between video game players and non-players. Kestenbaum and Weinstein (1985) found that video game playing teenagers did not differ from other youngsters on measures of neuroticism, extraversion or daydreaming. Regular players did indicate that they often played as a tension release, but no deep-seated personality idiosyncracies emerged for this group.

Some researchers have used teacher ratings of pupils to assess relationships between video game playing and children's personal characteristics. Linn and Lepper (1987) obtained school teacher ratings of academic achievement, personality characteristics, and behaviour patterns for children aged between nine and 11 years. Children who were more regular players of video games were also the ones rated higher by their teachers in terms of being impulsive and lower in terms of academic achievement. There was no indication that children who played video games a lot had fewer friends or were less socially skilled, however.

Arousal, Competence and Pleasure

The intrinsic appeal of video games to young people is likely to derive from several factors. Some of these factors reside within the games themselves, while others are characteristics of the individuals who play them. Earlier reported research indicated that video games can invoke a number of different emotional reactions among players (Kaplan and Kaplan 1981). Particular emotional reactions are likely to be linked to specific types of content and forms of presentation of events in video games. Equally, though, individuals endowed with a particular personality profile may be predisposed to react powerfully to certain content and form attributes. The way players react to video games may not simply be a matter of personality or type of game. Emotional responses to video games may be linked also to how well the game is played, with more skilled players getting more intrinsic satisfaction from playing.

Nelson and Carlson (1985) conducted two experiments with male American high school and junior high school students in an investigation of determinants of preferences for driving-type games and the effects of extended playing with these games on players' moods and motivation to continue playing. Four games were studied: these were *Death Race* and *Demolition Derby*, which simulated violent, antisocial driving behaviour and *Night Driver* and *Le Mans* which simulate skilled prosocial driving behaviour. The latter two games presented a road course that must be skilfully driven to achieve a high score. Leaving the roadway immediately discontinues either of these games. With the first two games, the player must steer a surrogate vehicle so as to strike make-believe pedestrians or other vehicles. Striking a character called the Gremlin in *Death Race* evokes a groan followed by a grave marker, while ramming the car in *Demolition Derby* removes it from the roadway.

Preference for arcade games simulating aggressive behaviour was found to be independent of personality and mood. However, preferences were closely related to the performers' capabilities. Players who exhibited higher levels of skill preferred the more skill demanding games and those who showed less skill preferred aggression games, suggesting the operation of competency motivation in that the players preferred games appropriate to their level of skill.

One might reasonably expect the aggressive symbolism and surrogate violence characterizing *Death Race* and *Demolition Derby* to lead to negative affective reactions greater than those arising from the nonviolent *Le Mans* and *Night Driver*. On the other hand, it is possible that engaging in *Demolition Derby* and *Death Race* will result in a greater cathartic release of aggressive impulses. While this seems unlikely because cathartic effects appear to require the person to be angry at the time game play begins (Murray and Feshbach 1978; Doob and Wood 1972), if catharsis occurs it should produce positive effects on mood and motivation of the *Death Race* and *Demolition Derby* players.

The conclusion reached by Nelson and Carlson was that playing arcade games has an equivalent short-term effect on all personalities and that this effect is not greatly influenced by the content of the game that is played. Generally, the games that players prefer are those that tax but do not exceed their level of competence or skill. However, the display of competence is not without its costs and these are represented in a general deterioration of mood, which has its biases or at least an analogue in fatigue.

Summary

Following their introduction in the mid-1970s, video games quickly became very popular. Although holding some appeal for adults, children and teenagers took to arcade and home video games more than any other age group. Arcade video games became especially popular among teenage males. The early concerns that it was the games' intrinsically addictive qualities that were leading young people astray and conditioning them into spending excessive amounts of time and money on video games were dispelled by the findings of observational research that revealed that the significance of arcades resided in their role as social meeting places for teenagers. Indeed, many teenagers went to arcades primarily to meet and be with their friends rather than to play video games, and for much of the time spent there, they did not actually play the games themselves, but either watched others playing or simply talked and hung out with others of their own age group.

Video games have generally held greater appeal for boys than for girls. The reasons for this are several (Dominick 1984; Morlock, Yando and Nigolean 1985; Kiesler, Sproull and Eccles 1985). In part the male dominance stems from a general perception that playing video games is more a masculine than a feminine activity (Surrey 1982; Schie and Wiegman 1996). This view is further reinforced by the dominant themes of the games that have clearly been directed more at boys than girls (Braun *et al.* 1986). This gender difference is then further exacerbated by the fact that as more regular players, boys also become more accomplished and more skilled exponents of video game play than girls. Girls can nevertheless make up this lost ground if they are given the encouragement to play these games for themselves (Subrahmanyam and Greenfield 1994).

Attempts to find out if the playing of video games and competence at playing are influenced by personality factors have produced relatively few positive results so far. There have been no indications, for instance, that children who play video games are more withdrawn or less gregarious than other children, or that they are less bright (Gibb *et al.* 1983; McClure and Mears 1984, 1986). There has been some suggestion that video game players, particularly females ones, with longer playing experience may also be more achievement oriented (Gibb *et al.* 1983).

Video games can generate mood changes in youngsters, however. Their interactive nature can invoke a considerable degree of concentration and involvement on the part of players, and generate a range of emotional reactions (Kaplan and Kaplan 1981). These reactions may vary with the theme, content type and presentation features which characterize particular games (Nelson and Carlson 1985). Later on in this book, we will find out whether video games can go beyond the generation of certain moods to produce changes in behaviour.

Chapter Three

Addiction and Dependency

The notion that the use of computers can become either a compelling habit or even an additive behaviour that takes over a person's life and is difficult to kick has been the focus of interest since computers and computer programming began to achieve greater prominence in various walks of life in the 1970s. One view was that computer programming could generate endless fascination for some people and cast an almost narcotic spell over them (Martin and Norman 1970). Furthermore, computer users generally attracted a rather disparaging image of dishevelled individuals with obsessional personalities and lacking in social skills. Such individuals would forego food and sleep for hours on end as their attention became totally focused on the computer screen (Weizenbaum 1976).

This computer dependency was regarded as compulsive behaviour, driven not by some intellectual need, but as a reaction to a challenge to the programmer's power to control the computer. One writer distinguished between 'compulsive' programmers and 'professional' programmers. The former were regarded as spending their time producing aimless, lengthy and poorly documented programs, of little use to anyone, while the latter used the computer as a tool to solve practical problems (Weisenbaum 1976). Turning his attention to arcade and computer games, the same writer believed that computerized games, especially ones with violent themes, could engender 'psychic numbing'. Violence in computer games was rated as far more subversive than violence on television because it engaged the participant interactively (Weizenbaum 1984). The same fears surfaced in Britain at the time these comments were being in America, as a Bill was laid before Parliament entitled the 'Control of Invaders and other Electronic Games' (Hansard 1981). Although the Bill was defeated it served to crystallize growing public disquiet about possible side-effects of this rapidly growing new home entertainment phenomenon.

This concern was particularly acute in the context of alleged consequences of regular computer game usage for children. Some observers have concluded that computer dependency among children may be potentially harmful to them in a variety of ways. Waddilove (1984) suggested that children could learn nothing about the world from the isolated use of the computer. Levy (1984) believed that their use could be causally linked with introversion. Weizenbaum (1984) suggested that games players could become psychically numbed. Brod (1984) argued that children's ability to learn would become distorted. He saw the use of the computer as providing a convenient refuge from stress, but by cutting the child off from other activities, it could prevent the development of well-rounded personalities. Another side-effect of strong computer or video game dependency is that in their desperation to play these games more and more, young people may turn to crime to obtain the money to maintain the habit. Loftus and Loftus (1983) reported one such case involving a 13-year-old boy in Des Moines, Iowa, who became a serial burglar in order to support his *Pac-Man* habit.

Another side-effect of habitual video game playing is that it may lead on to the development of gambling habits (Fisher 1994; Huff and Collinson 1987). Some of this evidence is speculative and perhaps the clearest explanation for a link stems from the fact that young people who begin playing with video games obtain their first exposure to fruit machines which are situated near by in an arcade. Griffiths (1995) reported a small study of eight self-confessed addicted adolescent fruit machine gamblers. With regard to video game machines, half the group had played them at some point. While they generally held the view that there was little or no obvious relationship between fruit machines and video game machines, those who used to play video games acknowledged that they started playing fruit machines as a result of their proximity to video game machines in arcades. Their initial exposure to fruit machines followed from their initial involvement with video game machines.

Shotton (1989) reported from her interviews with child users that the computer was used as a respite from stressful situations by some young players, but there was little evidence to suggest that such behaviours were caused by the computer itself. While individuals who exhibited what she termed 'computer dependency', did tend to exhibit less of an interest in physical or social activities, the use of the computer represented one aspect of their interest in more intellectually stimulating pastimes. A similar picture was painted by Simpson (1983) who noted that 'computer addiction' was a response to deficiencies elsewhere in life and deduced that such an activity could be in the child's best interest. Nicholson (1984) believed computer addiction to be symptomatic of needs not met elsewhere, and in addition felt it to be preferable to many other activities and no more socially isolating than watching television.

Can Video Games Become Addictive?

One of the most stinging criticisms of video games is that they can become addictive (Anderson and Ford 1986). To determine whether or not the degree to which players feel compelled to play computer or video games is an addiction, it is necessary to establish what a condition such as 'addiction' really means in this context (Griffiths 1996). One view is that being addicted to video games is like any other form of addictive behaviour. Being addicted means that players display a compulsive behavioural involvement with the games, accompanied by a lack of interest in other activities. As with other types of addiction, any attempts to stop the behaviour produces severe withdrawal symptoms (Soper and Miller 1983). Other writers have chosen to talk in terms of computer or video game 'dependency' rather than 'addiction', which may be applied to distinguish a particular category of person for whom playing with such games is not simply a major pre-occupation, but also serves special social and psychological functions in their lives that sets them apart from other computer or video game players (Shotton 1989).

Research has been carried out with adults and children to find out whether computer addiction or dependency really occurs and what form it takes. Evidence for addiction or dependency stems from an indication that playing video games eats into time spent with other activities to an extreme degree. Thus, any findings that indicate that video game playing does not submerge all other pursuits tend to weaken the argument for the games having addictive qualities. So far, much of the evidence from research is not strongly suggestive of video game addiction occurring to any great extent.

There have been conflicting opinions offered as to why computer or video games may generate dependency. One factor may be found in the inherent nature of the games themselves (Loftus and Loftus 1983).

A study carried out using an older generation of video games concluded that although a small number of people were in danger of becoming dependent, it was a harmless dependence (Shotton 1989). In the 1990s, however, construction of video games with increasingly realistic graphics and their requirement for complex skills on the part of players, may have increased the likelihood that these games could generate a powerful psychological dependence among certain types of individual. One of the problems in establishing whether computers can generate addiction or dependency among users is how such effects can be operationally defined. Indicators of such effects have taken the form of observations of players of computer and video games in arcades and the extent to which their attention is focused on the games rather than on other distractions; measures of the impact computer or video game usage can have upon other activities; the tendency of individuals to exhibit desperate patterns of behaviour in order to create opportunities for computer or video game play; and self-attributed dependency. The findings that derive from these different research perspectives have not, so far, yielded a consistent body of evidence.

Observations made of video game play behaviour in arcades have failed to show any firm support for the notion of addiction (Michaels 1993). The flow of business through arcades has been found to vary significantly with the occurrence of competing events that are more attractive to young people or that place constraints on discretionary time (e.g. school).

The suggestion that video game playing takes children and teenagers away from participating in more educational or sporting pursuits (e.g. Egli and Meyers 1984; Professional Association of Teachers 1994) is not borne out by contrary indications that video game players may be encouraged to read a great deal because of the very large number of magazines targeted at players (Griffiths 1996) and by findings indicating that video game players may be more likely than non-players to engage in sports (Phillips *et al.* 1995). With the latter finding, however, sportiness was less commonplace among the heaviest video game players.

Indirect evidence of how desperate youngsters can become to play video games, once hooked on them, has derived from findings that some may resort to stealing money to play arcade games or to buy new games cartridges for home video games (Klein 1984; Keepers 1990; Griffiths and Hunt 1993). Others may go without food, by forfeiting their lunch money to pay for video games (McClure and Mears 1984) or play truant from school to play (Keepers 1990; Griffiths and Hunt 1993). Signs of withdrawal symptoms such as increased irritability when unable to play have also been found (Griffiths and Hunt 1993; Rutkowska and Carlton 1994).

One intriguing illustration of an extreme case of what appears to be computer addiction came to be known as *Space Invaders* obsession. A small number of men, each about to be married, were observed to exhibit a significant increase in amount of time spent playing *Invaders* during the last few weeks preceding their wedding day. Apparently, in one case, the groom even insisted that the honeymoon be postponed for a few hours, enabling him to get in a few more games (Ross, Finestone and Lavin 1982).

Computer Game Addiction: An International Phenomenon?

There is international evidence that video games do not preoccupy children and teenagers to the exclusion of other pursuits. Brooks (1983) interviewed 973 young people in video arcades in southern California. He found some who felt compelled to play, but they were in a minority. In fact, around half of those he interviewed were playing games less than half the time they were in the arcade. The rest of the time they were socialising. Arcades provided a social gathering place for these young people.

In a different approach, Mitchell (1985) had 20 American families keep diaries for one week each month for five months after getting a video game set. If the games were addictive, this should have been reflected in long hours spent playing, particularly since the games could be played at home without spending money on them at an arcade. However, Mitchell found that the game sets were used an average of 42 minutes a day per family—and many of these families included more than one child, as well as parents who played. This was hardly indicative of an addictive pattern, especially when compared with the amount of time spent watching television.

In Japan, research among kindergarten children (aged three to five years) examined how much time they devoted to playing video games and doing other things. Playing time increased with age, but for most of the children there was a ceiling of around one hour a day. This increase in video game playing was more characteristic of boys than girls. Only a few cases of extreme levels of video playing (five or more hours a day) were reported. Generally, there was no evidence that video game playing interfered with making friends and playing with other children (Shimai, Masuda and Kishimoto 1990).

In the Netherlands, Schie and Wiegman (1996) found that playing video games did not appear to be at the expense of children's social integration. Girls who played video games reported that they felt more lonely. An American study followed a group of individuals who were reportedly hooked on video games over a period of five years and compared them with individuals who did not play video games. Computer dependent individuals were often highly intelligent, motivated and achieving people. Teenagers who were purportedly addicted to video games did well educationally, with many going to university and then into good jobs (Shotton 1989). These findings, however, may not necessarily reflect the kinds of reactions video game playing today can produce. The period studied by Shotton covered the early days of video games, since when games have become technically more advanced, require greater skill and are more involving. These features could make them potentially more 'addictive' than the old style games (Griffiths 1996).

What is the Nature of Addictiveness?

If video games are addictive, how does this process work? A number of theories exist about how video game addiction could come about. McIlwraith (1990) proposed four theoretical models to explain television addiction which Griffiths (1996) adapted to explain addiction to video games:

(1) Video game addiction is a function of the video game's effects on imagination and fantasy life, with people who play these games excessively having poor imaginations.

(2) Video game addiction is a function of the video game's effects on arousal level, such that people who play video games excessively do so either for their arousing or calming effects.

(3) Video game addiction is a manifestation of oral, dependent or addictive personality, with excessive playing being caused by inner personality factors rather than any external stimulation which derives from these games.

(4) Video game addiction is linked to a distinct pattern of uses of gratifications associated with video games, with players enjoy the physical act of playing or playing to alleviate boredom (p. 11).

Is Personality Related to Computer Game Addiction?

Accusations leveled against computer and video games that they are potentially harmful because they are addictive, in the sense that a drug may be addictive, carries the implication that all who play with these games may be susceptible to such influences. Observations in other contexts have indicated, however, that addictive behaviour, whatever the context, is not simply a reaction to sets of circumstances, but often represents a predisposition associated with certain types of personality (Griffiths 1995). Is there any evidence that certain personality types among children and teenagers are more prone to develop and exhibit an 'addictive' quality toward their involvement with computer and video games?

For some writers, the personality of the computer user was a key factor underpinning the likelihood that they would exhibit addictive or dependent tendencies (McCorduck 1979). Favaro (1982) did not believe that computer or video games could themselves be addictive. He did hypothesize, however, that children with pre-existing emotional disorders might well manifest compulsive behaviours of one sort or another.

In the context of computer programming, the potency of computers to produce user dependency was thought, by some writers, to derive from the computer being treated almost as another person by the obsessional programmer. The computer may take on an anthropomorphized quality and evoke emotional responses from people which are not dissimilar from genuine human interactions (Shallis 1984). Another observer noted that the computer 'offers us the illusion of total control, and it appears to give us its full attention, often being immediately responsive to every remark addressed to it ...' (Boden 1981). Thus, not only is the computer like another person, but it may often behave in a much more positive and friendly way towards the user than a real person. Recently, the computer as 'being' analogous to a life form, has become more explicit manifest in the form of the *Tamagotchi* product, which represents a kind of miniature, electronic pet or child, in constant need of attention from its owner.

A worrying development could occur if the computer user's need for power over the computer transferred to their desired relationships with other people (Thimbleby 1979). The focus upon the power-related needs of computer users ignored the fact that interaction with computers also represented a playful and light-hearted pastime for many. This was a true reflection of the nature of computer usage as least as often as the darker side of the need for control (Frude 1983).

So far, the idea that certain children, by virtue of their personality profile, might be more predisposed to computer or video game addiction has failed to find consistent empirical support. Gibb *et al.* (1983) measured over 200 video game players, including teenagers and young adults up to the age of 34, on a variety of personality dimensions including obsessiveness/compulsiveness. No indication was found that more obsessional or compulsive individuals tended to spend greater amounts of time playing video games.

Further research is needed to establish theoretical explanations for any relationships between computer usage and human personality characteristics. Recent research with young adults has indicated, for example, that arousal levels can rise during video game play, particularly among regular players and that this may motivate repeated playing (Griffiths and Dancaster 1995). Players were divided into Type A and Type B personality types, with the former expected to exhibit greater increases in arousal during video game play than the latter. Findings indicated that Type A players did become more aroused by playing video games than did Type B players, and that this might render Type A's more susceptible to video game addiction. Other factors such as fantasizing ability, addictive personality or uses and gratifications remain to be properly investigated.

Perhaps the most detailed published study of computer dependency and addiction that also examined ways of distinguishing different personality types in terms of the particular patterns of dependency exhibited by computer users was conducted by Shotton (1989). She conducted research with university students and school children to trace their inherent characteristics as computer users, the motives for their computer involvement and the existence among them of computer 'dependency', which she distinguished from 'addiction'.

Initial interviews with a small group of five undergraduate students yielded qualitative data that shed some light on these matters. These individuals spent about 30 hours of spare time each week on the computer. Some of the computer sessions were quite long, on occasions lasting for more than ten hours at a stretch. These individuals acknowledged that they were 'hooked' on computers. They engaged in programming activities of their own and gained considerable enjoyment from developing their own programmes, especially from the activity of 'debugging' them to ensure they worked as intended. The views offered here bore a striking resemblance to the observations made earlier by Weizenbaum (1976) for whom computer dependent programmers were characterized by gaining most pleasure from interacting with computers, rather than from producing something functional or useful.

The five individuals interviewed by Shotton also reportedly played computer games, and particularly enjoyed elaborate adventure games which they found more intellectually stimulating than most arcade games. These computer 'junkies' also enjoyed 'hacking'—gaining unauthorised access to computer systems via the networks.

Acknowledging the limitations of a small qualitative study, Shotton (1989) extended her research with larger adult and child samples. To obtain more adult subjects, she advertised for participants in a study of computer usage from further afield and obtained 180 initial responses from volunteers who were subsequently sent a questionnaire which among other things, asked them whether they were 'hooked on' computers. A total of 151 responses were received, among whom 121 considered themselves to be computer dependent. Of these 95 also agreed that they would be willing to be further interviewed.

A battery of questionnaires, tests, scales and interview schedules were developed by Shotton, which examined computer programming, hardware and software interests, leisure activities, attitudes to computers, attitudes to parents, personality factors, and assessment of time spent computing. Other background details about respondents were also collected. Standardized personality tests were used, including the Sixteen Personality Factor Questionnaire (16PF) (IPAT 1979) and the Group Embedded Figures Test (GEFT) (Oltman *et al.* 1971). These instruments were posted to respondents in succession, yielding progressively lower response rates.

The group of computer *dependents* were compared with two further control samples of computer *Owners* who were not judged to be computer dependent, and *Non-owners* of computers. Among the 'dependents' more were single (61) than married (40). A handful were separated, divorced or widowed. They were mostly aged under 40. Around half were aged under 30. They exhibited a mixed range of educational achievements. Some were graduates, others were not. Fewer dependents were married than within the control samples. Some dependents considered their parents to have been older than usual, leading to a more conservative restricted life-style. A high proportion of dependents were also first born children (50 per cent). The majority of dependents and their fathers had occupations within the areas of science and technology.

In another part of her study interviews were conducted by Shotton with school children to establish computer dependency tendencies, children's attitudes towards and use of computers in the classroom and outside; and the nature of school computing. Some teachers were also interviewed about their opinions towards computers and the sort of training they themselves had had in computer usage. Data were obtained through questionnaires sent to 85 secondary schools, to the main computer studies teacher. Forty-one teachers replied, and 23 interviews followed. Of the 23 schools visited, 11 teachers believed that they had taught children who exhibited characteristic symptoms of computer dependency, and between them reported 26 boys and one girl as such.

Computer dependent children were regarded as intelligent but socially inadequate in some way. Most of these pupils were considered to have experienced social difficulties before using computers. The findings here were consistent with comments made by the small group of undergraduates interviewed by Shotton.

Teachers reported that greater likelihood of becoming computer dependent was associated with boys who held a generally more immature attitude towards their work, and who treated the computer as a toy rather than as a tool. They were also considered to be more likely than girls to have just one serious hobby. These facets led boys with poor social skills to become 'obsessive' about computing.

In general boys were more interested in computers than girls. Reasons offered by teachers were manifold. First, computing was linked to mathematics and science subjects within schools, subjects that have been traditionally viewed as 'masculine', and as a consequence female prejudices and lack of confidence in these subjects were transferred directly to computer studies. Computer studies teachers were invariably male (ratio of 3:1), a finding corroborated by other studies (see Saunders 1975; Weiner 1980; Ward 1983, 1985).

Female teachers were often as disaffected by new technology as their students, and were less likely to own a home computer themselves. They lacked familiarity with them. Thus, girls did not have as much access to same-sex role models or indeed encouragement from adult members of their own sex as did boys. There was inadequate training of teachers in the use of computers which meant that it remained in the domain of computer studies, where teachers were mostly male.

The research conducted by Shotton and by others indicated that boys enjoyed programming and learning about the hardware, while girls wanted to use the computer as a tool without wishing to learn to program did not see the computer as intrinsically interesting. Computer studies was not seen as relevant to girls' lives (Equal Opportunities Commission 1983; Forrest 1984; Ward 1983). Boys tended to be confident in their dealings with computers. They rarely planned their programs adequately, but enjoyed the necessary debugging that resulted. Girls tended to plan carefully, perhaps through fear of using the computer, and expected the program to run at the first attempt. The weaker enthusiasm for computer-usage among girls stemmed to a significant degree from this subject being labelled and generally regarded as a boys subject. Other observers have noted that girls have a tendency to opt out of 'masculine' subjects that they find difficult (Keys and Ormerod 1976).

In the context of computer usage, many boys had more experience in using new technology out of school (Shotton 1989). Boys are more likely to believe that computers are easy to use while girls are more likely to question their ability in this area. Failure that girls show little enthusiasm to correct and the need to engage in activities such as the debugging of programs, which many girls feel uncomfortable about, has further confirmed this belief among girls, often leading to the development of a form of learned helplessness and poor achievement motivation where computers are concerned (Dweck *et al.* 1978; Fennema 1981).

The teachers interviewed by Shotton (1989) concluded that computing was taught in secondary schools in a manner found to attract boys and alienate girls. Girls from single-sex schools and girls of Asian origin were exceptions to this rule. With Asian girls, there was a generally more positive attitude towards computers, which was partly reinforced by the importance attached to all education by Asian families. In general, however, the British system of teaching was seen by teachers to discriminate between the sexes.

Shotton administered questionnaires about computing to a sample of 2720 children, and 1656 were returned. The questionnaire was completed by 886 boys and 770 girls from four secondary schools). Nearly 45 per cent of boys and 33 per cent of girls spontaneously listed computing and/or mathematics as favourite subjects—a significant difference between the sexes, though a higher proportion of endorsements from girls than would have been expected on the basis of teachers' evidence. Boys were also more likely to use computer clubs at lunchtimes than were girls. 53 per cent of boys compared with 32 per cent of girls had computers at home.

Owners of computers were significantly more interested in computing than non-owners. This was true of girl owners as well as boy owners. Among non-owners, there was no difference between boys and girls in the number who wished that they owned a computer. Among computer owners, boys reported higher levels of usage than did girls, with 30 per cent of boys and just 6 per cent of girls claiming to use the computer more than ten hours a week.

In general, girls were more likely to require a useful end-product from their computing efforts and expected computers to be more controllable and more easily used than, in fact, they were. Together with being more inhibited by the technology, they were more likely to doubt their capabilities to use the computer and were more easily frustrated when programs did not run at the first attempt.

The Nature of Computing Experiences

Among the adult sample, Shotton (1989) compared reports of *dependents* and *owners* who were non-dependents. Both groups appeared to have had equal opportunities to use computers in working or academic environments. Dependents were more likely to have purchased their own computer earlier than owners. Dependents were not deterred by unfriendly systems. They were keen to own a computer as early as possible and learn as much as they could about it. Owners were more likely to have had their interest sparked by using computers in a functional setting.

Dependents did tend to spend more hours on the computer than owners. Dependents were also more likely to spend extended spells at the computer. Dependents devoted more of their spare time to computing. Dependents would spend more time with their computers if they did not have to sleep or go to work. Dependents were characterized in particular by a greater need to understand their computer and to be able to control it. Non-dependent computer owners were more likely than dependants to have bought their computers for functional rather than self-educational reasons. They were also more likely to have received formal training in programming and used this training when programming at home. Dependents liked to find out about programming for themselves, and were less likely to pre-plan their programming activities. Dependants had a need to challenge and understand the work of others, and enjoyed code-breaking activities. Computer dependents and non-dependent computer owners had different beliefs and attitudes about computers. Owners saw the computer as a functional, problem-solving tool. Dependents purchased computers in order to find out more about them.

One signifier of computer dependency is the extent to which it takes over from all other activities. Dependent users neglect other social and leisure activities, and may even forget to eat or sleep because they are so bound up with the things they are doing with their computer. Is there any evidence, however, that some individuals are more prone to develop such patterns of behaviour than others? Shotton (1989) asked whether computer dependency was most likely to occur in individuals with few other interests.

In her survey of adult computer users, those designated as computer dependents frequently mentioned having mechanical and electronics hobbies and expressed a keen interest in such subjects as science fiction and music. Dependents were significantly more likely than non-dependents to mention hobbies such as technology, science, mathematics, and were more often likely to regard computing as a hobby. In addition, however, dependants socialised less often than non-dependents.

Results showed that there were great differences in the hobbies of interest to the dependants, the owners and the non-owners, with the two computer groups sharing some interests, the two control groups sharing others, but with few being shared by the dependants and the non-owners. Computer owners, whether exhibiting signs of computer dependency or not, were more likely than computer non-owners to like games and puzzles, and computing and electronics. The two computer-user groups were also more likely to enjoy practical crafts.

Dependents were generally less interested in sports, particularly competitive ball games. Finally, dependents did not enjoy socializing very much. If they did do any of this it tended to be with small gatherings of like-minded people.

One of the key characteristics of regular computer users was that they generally held more positive attitudes towards computers than did non-owners. Computer owners obtained considerable satisfaction from using computers, so were more comfortable than non-owners when sitting in front of a console and found playing around with computer a relaxing pastime.

Individuals who exhibited computer dependency enjoyed computers as a form of relaxation more than any other group.

Distinguishing Psychological Characteristics of Computer Dependency

One of the aims of this investigation was to identify whether there were any defining background characteristics that might underpin computer dependency. Did computer dependents differ from non-dependent computer owners and users in their family upbringing, relationships with parents, social networks, and so on, which might in turn be linked with their personality profile? In their replies computer dependents did not appear to consider that their family upbringing was out of the ordinary. Nevertheless, many described their fathers as cold and distant. Indeed, computer dependents seemed to regard both parents more often as distant, compared with non-dependents computer users. Computer dependents' descriptions of their relationships with their parents indicated that these were fairly poor and lacking in real affection. Research elsewhere has indicated that deprivation in fathering, either through absence or low interaction, has been seen to lead to fearfulness in social situations (Spelke *et al.* 1973), to lack of trust in others (Santrock 1970) and to obsessive compulsive neurosis (Tseng-Wen-Sheng 1973). Deprivation of a nurturing father may lead to a lack of maturity and self confidence (Bronfenbrenner 1961).

To provide further evidence on distinguishing features of computer dependents, Shotton asked her respondents to describe what kinds of personalities they considered themselves to have and also had them complete standardized personality tests. Computer dependents considered themselves to be isolated, introverted, shy and misunder-stood. They also rated themselves as more curious and materialistic and less attractive than did other groups. In self-reports, dependents reported themselves as being less content, more unfulfilled and un-happy than controls.

On the basis of standardized test responses, computer dependents were found to be more field independent than non-dependents. Field independence is associated with a developed sense of separate identity and selfhood, among people who are unlikely to revise their views because of social influences and attitudes (Bell 1955). In times of stress such people tend to use the specific defence mechanism of isolation from others in order to separate feelings from thoughts and ideas (Witkin et al. 1962), and at the cost of an emotional life place great reliance upon intellectualization.

On the 16 PF, dependents scored higher on conservative/experiment-ing, practical/imaginative. They were prone to fantasize and become absorbed in ideas. Dependants scored higher in terms of being stubborn and competitive. The dependents' need for solitary, intellectual pursuits, giving little regard to emotions, other people or everyday practicalities indicated that they had discovered and developed methods of living which were in keeping with their personalities and interests.

Types of Computer Dependency

In addition to identifying whether there were any defining personality characteristics associated with computer dependency, Shotton (1989) also searched for sub-groups among computer dependents. She divided her interviewees (a) according to the time spent on their home com-puters and (b) according to their preferred computing activities. From this analysis three types were identified among those respondents designated as computer dependents: (1) networkers who rarely if ever wrote their own programs, but who principally used computers as a means of communication via networks with other databases; (2) workers—all of whom stated that their computing was work-related; and (3) explorers —who stated that they spent the majority of their time programming in an investigative, self-educational and exploratory manner. These groups did not differ in terms of sex, marital status, educational levels, and so on. They were all interested in science and technology rather than the arts. All owned similar quantities of software and similar numbers in each group had attempted hacking.

Networkers differed from the other two in holding more positive attitudes towards other people. They considered themselves less shy and more comfortable socially. They experienced fewer difficulties in their relationships with the opposite sex, than did other dependents. They also seemed to have enjoyed better relationships with their parents. They were more likely to view the computer as a hobby or toy than the other dependents.

Some of the networkers devoted much of their time to playing adventure games, especially MUDs (Multi-user Dungeons and Dragons, now known as Multi-user Domains), a very elaborate, interactive game, at that time played via the Essex University DEC-10 mainframe computer. MUD is a text-based game of fantastic scenarios through which the players have to find their way in pursuit of treasure, solving puzzles along the way. Players include wizards, mortals, goblins and sorcerers, using swords and magic wands to defeat rivals in the pursuit of their goals (Machin 1984). Two or three dozen people, with access to this computer via their modems, could play MUD simultaneously. Often the game had to be played late at night when the university's computer was not being heavily used for work purposes. Players could communicate with each other, cooperate in tackling adventure scenarios, or compete against one another. Players could also develop their own spin on a story by creating new characters, obstacles and situations, twists and turns in the plot, which other players would then face as new challenges (Reid 1995). This network acted as a source of relationships. Shotton even observed that it served as a virtual dating agency for people who may never meet one another.

Shotton found no evidence that networkers' personalities had been affected detrimentally by their use of computers. There were suggestions that some friendships had been forged with people with whom contact had been established over the net. This impression was consistent with observations made by Brod (1984) who believed networks to be the ideal medium for gaining understanding and companionship from like-minded individuals and discussed their use as dating agencies, and Frude (1983) who believed that the isolated and the disabled were likely to benefit greatly from their use. The positive aspects of networking were also recognised by Boden (1984) and Kiesler *et al.* (1984), who believed that the use of networks could be liberating for the more socially shy, and because of the anonymity afforded could promote intimacy and reduce self-consciousness. In addition, Edinger and Patterson (1983) felt that the lack of social cues involved in the communication would make it more egalitarian, and allow the inhibited to become more assertive in their interactions with others.

The games playing and hacking undertaken by Shotton's networkers also seemed to encourage social interaction, although games playing has been reported to have detrimental effects upon people (see Weizenbaum 1976 and Favaro 1982). However, when Gibb *et al.* (1983) undertook research to determine whether this was so, they found no indication that games playing encouraged social isolation even when playing solitary games, as ideas and games were often exchanged with others. They found that their 280 subjects showed less obsessive-compulsive behaviour than usual for the established norms. They concluded that this was due to the fact that the games required flexibility of responses, not mastery of a rigid response pattern; a fact which is especially true of adventure games such as MUDs that were of especial interest to the networkers. In an earlier study, Nicholson (1984) recognized that the instant feedback and feelings of control engendered when playing games could be psychologically very rewarding, and give an increase in self-esteem and belief in one's own competence and abilities. Similar theories were expressed by McClure and Mears (1984) who also showed that computer games were especially enjoyed by young males who liked challenges, (and in addition liked science fiction), and that adventure games were of greater interest than arcade games to those with high intelligence.

'Workers' in the Shotton classification were all male, and concentrated on writing programmes with a specific end-product in mind. Many were self-employed, with jobs where computing was a central component. Many were ambitious careerists. They would spend more time at the computer than other groups, because it was their work as well as a hobby. They were more likely to use commercial business software and more likely to frown upon hacking. The work ethic was important to this group. On the 16PF they were revealed as being more conscientious and controlled. They were also highly emotionally disciplined, determined and responsible individuals.

The 'Explorers' were more interested in the use of computers for exploratory and self-educational purposes. They epitomized the characteristics of those described as computer junkies by Weizenbaum (1976). They yearned for comprehension, understanding and mastery of the computer world. Debugging programs took up much of their time and gave them great pleasure. They also needed to understand the hardware, and not just the software. They were significantly less likely to spend time in personal communication with others. They revelled in jargon and were not put off by the poor manuals provided with much computer software. The computer was often regarded as a friend or companion. Explorers were shy and introverted, and less emotionally stable than the workers. They had had poor relationships with their parents, especially their fathers.

Turkle (1984) recognized that the computer dependent person used the computer as compensation for dissatisfaction in other areas of life, but she believed this to be with politics and work, neither of which were mentioned by Shotton's explorer category. Turkle also believed that computing was taken up during teenage years by boys who had difficulty relating to girls, with the computer allowing them to gain competency and control.

Turkle divided the dedicated users into two groups, the hobbyists and hackers (using the term hacker in a global sense, rather than specifically to refer to breaking into other systems). She believed that they undertook different tasks for different reasons. The hobbyist was seen as a risk-taker, who endowed the computer with magical qualities, and liked to make small changes to their programs to see what would happen. The hackers, on the other hand, she saw as needing reassurance by maintaining total control over the computer, by the use of assembler languages and mastery of the hardware. These two divisions were not all apparent from her interviews. The explorers showed both sets of characteristics very strongly; they were not mutually exclusive. They were only able to gain complete control over the computer by deliberately taking risks and observing the outcome, and one of the main satisfactions gained from their computing was that it allowed them to take risks within the confines of a safe environment, while simultaneously keeping control of the whole system. The computer and its behaviour. however bizarre, could not frighten or intimidate them; it was comprehensible and logical, unlike people.

Good Effects or Bad Effects?

In its overview of issues connected with the growth in popularity and widespread use of computer and video games, Chapter One highlighted a number of concerns that have been voiced about computer usage, which have generally been associated with allegations of unwanted side-effects of computer usage, especially among children and teenagers. One particular set of worries has been reserved for the intellectual, emotional and social side-effects of excessive computer-related play. These effects have been explored in more detail in the current chapter. While computer dependency has been identified by some researchers as a behavioural profile associated with computer usage, individuals who exhibit this tendency also often exhibit introverted personalities and poor social skills. While these personal attributes may not be caused by devoting large amounts of time to playing with computers, any suggestion that individuals who display such personalities use computers as a means of escape or a cloak to hide behind carries with it the implication that computers will not make things better for them. Sooner or later they must face up to reality and develop the skills and competencies needed to operate effectively in the wider social environment.

In contrast to this view, there are those who believe that computers may provide a constructive solution to some of the social problems faced by shy and withdrawn individuals. Instead of drawing them further into a technological cocoon, shielding them from unpleasant realities of the real world with which they are reluctant to deal head-on, computers may provide an alternative channel through which they can express themselves and establish social networks, while functioning with a medium with which they feel comfortable and confident. Confirming this alternative view, Shotton (1989) found that the computer dependent individuals she studied had achieved some very positive benefits from their computing activities. In some instances, these benefits had been able to compensate for a lack of development in other areas of their lives. Such individuals had often had difficulties maintaining social relationships. The use of the computer had given them the opportunity to reproduce an interaction that mirrored their own modes of thinking, and in addition many felt that they were able to communicate more easily with others. The use of networks enabled them to interact with people of like mind with whom they were able to share mutual interests, and such activity was felt to have expanded their range of friendships.

Believing that computers are 'machines to think with, not things which think' and because of their non-human characteristics, Pateman (1981) believed that computers have many advantages when used for educational purposes by allowing learning to take place more easily and positively. He believed that the use of the computer eliminated the 'unnecessary obstacles to thinking, creativity, invention, discovery and learning' which tend to occur frequently with traditional methods of learning, where criticism may stifle the learner's enthusiasm. Computer learning takes place at the user's pace, matching abilities and current levels of knowledge, and because of lack of inhibition and judgment present within the interaction, computers are sometimes found to be easier to relate to than people. Computers do not criticize the person, merely the program they have written, thereby allowing self-criticism and development to take place. According to some commentators, the non-judgmental responses received when working at a computer may allow people to accept failure in a positive manner, while encouraging them to strive for other solutions (Papert 1972). Others believe that use of the computer could lead to greater problem-solving skills that can be applied elsewhere in life (Eisele 1981). The science fiction aspect of computing may lead regular computer users to think the impossible and then strive to attain it (Levy 1984).

Children especially may benefit from these outcomes. Turkle (1984) believed that personal programming could lead children to develop highly individualized styles of learning, rather than all being expected to conform to the same educational mould, allowing them to develop their own personal strengths, cognitive styles and personalities in a controlled but free manner. Chapter Four will examine in greater detail the potential cognitive benefits to children of their involvement with computers.

Networking with like-minded computer users has been reported to expand computer dependents' circle of friends. Work by Kiesler *et al.* (1987) demonstrated that networkers were found to be far less inhibited when using this method of communication than when face-to-face, and that more equality of participation was observed with less likelihood of one person being totally dominant in group communication. Whether these communication skills generalize to real interpersonal situations, has not been demonstrated. Such interaction, even though computer-mediated, has been regarded as being highly beneficial to the shy computer dependent person (Shotton 1989).

Contrary to producing further withdrawal into isolated amusement, thus exacerbating their introversion (Levy 1984) and not teaching them anything of any use to their dealings with the real world (Waddilove 1984), the use of computer games may well aid the development of social interaction, whether used educationally or as entertainment (see Loftus and Loftus 1983). This effect may result from playing with computer and video games, both in the home and beyond it. Egli and Meyers (1984) found that arcades acted as social centres and places for the development of friendship, in a similar manner to Shotton's dependents who made contact and friendships with others in order to share and copy games software.

Since playing computer games involves a challenge between the player and software, and not between the player and another person, computer games-playing was found to decrease competitiveness and to increase cooperativeness (Bowman 1982). It also provided an ideal environment for the development of competence, self-determination and status.

Shotton (1989) reported from her interviews with child users that the computer was used by some youngsters as a respite from stressful situations, but there was little evidence to suggest that such behaviours were caused by the computer itself. While individuals who display computer dependency may exhibit less of an interest in certain physical or social activities, the use of the computer represented one aspect of their interest in more intellectually stimulating pastimes, rather than a need to withdraw from social reality. In some senses, computer 'addiction' or 'dependency' may represent a response to deficiencies elsewhere in an individual's life, but playing with a computer could nevertheless be regarded as a positive activity enabling that person to express themselves through a medium they enjoyed using (Simpson 1983). In many ways, playing with a computer may be preferable to a whole range of other activities a socially isolated child might pursue (Nicholson 1984).

Chapter Four

Effects of
Video Games on Cognitive Skills

One of the early concerns about computer and video games, given their widespread popularity with young people, was that it might interfere with academic performance by offering a more attractive option than doing homework. The empirical evidence on this point has been mixed. Clearly if children were to spend all their time outside school playing with electronic games to the neglect of studying or other activities from which they might benefit intellectually or socially, this could not be thought to be a good thing. One early investigation found no correlation between use of microcomputers and academic performance (Dominick 1984), another study found that access to a computer outside school was positively linked to academic scores (Lockheed, Nielson and Stone 1983), while yet another found that home computer use was negatively related to how well a child performed at school (Braun *et al.* 1986). In the latter case, however, much seemed to depend on the nature of computer usage. Children who were involved in doing their own programming at home actually exhibited better academic performance. Although more associated with boys than girls, girls have been found to show greater appreciation for compulsory computer tuition in class than do boys (Braun *et al.* 1986). Girls also preferred operating computers in groups, reflecting their general preference for verbal and social activities (Arrindell 1983).

Not everyone believes that computer and video games are bad for children. There are some who believe that these games can have educational benefits. The idea that involvement with computers can have such beneficial side-effects is not new. Educators have acknowledged the potential of the computer to assist children to learn for at least 30 years. The concept of computer-assisted instruction (CAI) appeared in the 1960s. In one major project conducted in California, thousands of elementary school children were taught a variety of subjects with the assistance of computers. Exercises and tests in arithmetic, for example, were administered via computer consoles with which students interacted, and results were delivered at the end of each session. Computer-assisted instruction was also devised for a course of Russian, with instruction being received at computer terminals for 50 minutes a day, five days a week for an entire academic year. Indeed, CAI students performed better than non-CAI students taught with traditional methods (Suppes 1966; Atkinson and Wilson 1968). For some writers, the computer presented a potentially much more effective learning medium than television because it more actively engaged students in learning exercises (Papert 1980).

School computing has often come under fire for displaying a lack of purposiveness and academic justification, poor quality software and for showing gender bias towards boys (Nairman 1982; Sanders 1984; Seidel, Anderson and Hunter 1982; Stevens 1980). The growth of computers has been defended elsewhere for having many positive benefits (Gibb *et al.* 1983). Microcomputers and their accompanying software have been reported to engage and cultivate particular kinds of complex spatial cognitive learning (Ball 1978; Jones 1981; Kennedy, Bittner and Jones 1981; Lowery and Knirk 1983).

Computer and video games, as a form of computing, have also been thought to possess educational as well as entertainment value. While computers, in the CAI context, can be seen as conveyers of to-be-learned material, however, the educational potential of playing video games may take the form of enhancing the development of certain cognitive skills. These skills are invoked through video game play and are necessary to play the game successfully, embracing certain information processing strategies that are not only required by the game, but that may also be transferable to other information processing contexts. These other contexts may consist of other video games or other uses of computers (White 1992), or other non-computer information processing tasks (Greenfield 1994).

Computer games scenarios can provide contexts in which memory for certain types of content can be enhanced and taken beyond the performance level found after to-be-learned material was presented in a more standard taught lesson. Young children, aged four to seven years, have been found to show better memory for pictures displayed during a computer game than when presented in a lesson format (Oyen and Bebko 1996). The effectiveness of computer games in enhancing learning and memory for subject matter depends critically on the degree to which the to-be-learned material is integrated with the fantasy component of the game (Lepper 1985). In examining this phenomenon further, Oyen and Bebko (1996) distinguished between 'exogenous' games in which the learning content was only arbitrarily linked with the fantasy component of the game, and 'endogenous' games in which the to-be-learned content is intrinsically interrelated with the game itself. In their study, an endogenous game produced better subsequent picture content recall than did an exogenous game. One reason for this effect is that computer games can make learning more interesting (Corno and Mandinach 1983). As a consequence, they may try harder to overcome obstacles to learning and persist at difficult problems.

Children may therefore be able to learn through video games, even when playing for fun. This learning may occur incidentally whereby children who play video games also acquire certain skills that may be useful in the contexts of other applications of computers. One computer game designer has described the experience of playing with these games as a process of deconstruction, whereby players do not just simply learn how to play the game, but also learn the principles behind them to the extent where they may even uncover flaws in the design. In this way, '... a game should lift the player up to higher levels of understanding' (Crawford 1986: 16).

Video game technology, itself, has been adapted to more formal educational settings to assist with learning exercises. In the United States, for example, video games have been used successfully in the context of language teaching. Fredericksen and his colleagues (1982) developed a video game for educational purposes called *Speed*. This required a player to detect whether a target letter cluster was present within words that were presented in rapid succession. An example might be whether the letter cluster 'LER' is to be found in the word 'HUSTLER', to which the answer is 'yes', and whether it is to be found in the word 'HOUSEHOLD', to which the answer is 'no'. Such a task is fairly straightforward when you have plenty of time, but in the game itself, players were required to make many such judgments at a faster and faster pace as the game wore on. Errors would be signalled by a light coming on, and the word presentation rate was then decreased. Computer or video games as such are believed to motivate children to learn by rendering boring material more interesting, and can simplify tasks by providing children with further encouragement to persist (Hubbard 1991). Video games do not invariably work well, however, nor do they operate with equal success among all children. Some children perform better than others with this kind of learning.

Video games can pose challenges to children that require them to utilize specific cognitive skills, but in a context that makes learning fun. Such games work best if they present a clearly-defined goal or objective for the child to achieve, and offer enough uncertainty regarding outcomes at different points in play to provide a real challenge. Loftus and Loftus (1983) presented a theoretical example of one such game:

> ... imagine a computer game in which children read about a child hero who is given information about latitudes and longitudes and must use this information to solve the problem of rescuing other children from evil aliens who are holding hostages at various points around the globe. The player roams around the computer world seeking these hostages and is rewarded for each one found. Instead of being tedious, unconnected facts, existing only to be memorized in school, city locations constitute vital information, and the ability to locate the cities becomes a necessary skill for achieving the interesting goal of rescuing hostages. Moreover the goal is part of an intrinsic fantasy, involving a child hero with whom the child learners can strongly identify (1983: 126-27).

Since writing these remarks, computer games have emerged that offer this kind of intellectual challenge to players. A good example of this type of game is *Sim City*, a simulation that allows players to design their own city from scratch. Friedman (1995) describes the basic principles of this game:

> Beginning (in the basic scenario) with an undeveloped patch of land and an initial development fund, the player constructs a city by choosing where and what kind of power plants to build, zoning industrial, commercial and residential areas, laying down roads, mass transit and power lines, and building police stations, fire departments, and eventually airports, seaports, and stadiums, and so on. Although playing the game eventually comes to feel entirely intuitive, the system is quite complex ... Every action is assigned a price, and the player can only spend as much money as he or she has in the city treasury. The treasury begins at a basic amount and can be replenished yearly by taxes, the rate of which is determined by the player. As the player becomes more familiar with the system, she or he gradually develops strategies to encourage economic growth, build up the population of the

city, and score a higher 'approval rating' from the Sims. Which of these or other goals the player chooses to pursue, however, is up to the individual (1995: 80-81).

Children and teenagers may have many different reasons for wanting to play video games, but three particular factors were identified fairly early on as being of special importance: challenge, curiosity and fantasy (Malone 1981). The use of these components in the design of a video game could not only make the games more fun, but also more educational. Sutton-Smith (cf. Surrey 1982) argued that video games are a good influence because they give children access to state-of-the-art technology. It has also been argued similarly by Gordon (cf. Surrey 1982) that video games give children a sense of confidence and equips them with computer-related skills for the future, although there was no mention of what exactly these skills were.

It may also be intuitively argued that playing video games is an involving fantasy experience that can have spin-offs for children in their own lives. Since these interactive games can engage a child's attention in a powerful way, they can also regulate a child's arousal level, causing it to decrease by distracting the player's attention from real world problems or to increase it in a highly competitive game. Video games can prepare children to deal with real life situations under safer conditions, through simulation exercises. Finally, video games can boost a child's confidence when play is successful.

Video game simulations have been found to produce successful results in the training of adults (e.g. in the armed forces) in the application of certain psycho-motor skills (Nawrocki and Winner 1983; Carter, Kennedy and Bittner 1980; Jones 1981; Trachtman 1981). It has also been reported that US Navy officials frequent video arcades to recruit trainees with the promise that the Navy has a greater selection of better quality games on offer (Soper and Miller 1983).

The importance of establishing the nature and degree of any cognitive influences of video games upon children is underlined by evidence indicating that when they are available children begin to play these games at a very early age. Children as young as three have been found to acquire the skills to manipulate computer-based games (Strommen, Razavi and Medoff 1992). Rather than seeing them as a threat, some scholars who have studied video games closely, regard them as an aspect of modern culture to be embraced and utilized constructively.

A New Literacy

There was much discussion in the early 1980s about the new form of literacy that might emerge as a result of the mass introduction of microelectronic technologies such as video games (e.g. Compaine 1983). One feature of this computer literacy was thought to be the development of greater spatial reasoning and visualization abilities. Studies had already noted that the introduction of television produced significant gains in visual skills, termed 'television literacy' (Salomon 1979). Video games may be the next generation of media to produce subtle changes in mental skills.

There has been a great deal of speculation concerning the possible beneficial effects of video games. It has been widely proposed that video games can teach a range of cognitive skills, increase attention spans and concentration, and improve spatial visualization and eye-hand co-ordination. Ball (1978) claimed that video games can teach certain physical coordination skills, decision-making, following directions, and numerical and word recognition skills. He further suggested that video games could increase the attention span of players who had difficulty focusing on a single task for longer than a few minutes. Not only attention span, but also the ability effectively to divide visual attention between different tasks or aspects of a task can be cultivated through playing certain video games (Greenfield *et al.* 1994).

Video games can be thought of as being cultural artifacts (Greenfield 1994). As with other cultural artifacts, video games embody a particular symbol system. This means that video games have their own peculiar form of presenting things, they have their own structure, their own grammar. Learning how to use them and how to absorb information from them therefore requires a particular cognitive competence on the part of the individual. Just as experience in television viewing enables individuals to understand the conventions of presentation in different kinds of programmes, so also with video games, certain mental skills need to be acquired in order to play the games to an advanced level.

The skills needed to handle video games effectively have been referred to in some quarters as 'representational competence' (Sigel and Cocking 1977). This competence is concerned with the means and modalities by which we take in, transform, and transmit information. Bruner (1965 1966) developed a theory of three modes of representation and their role in development. This theory was really a theory of the development of representational competence (Greenfield 1994). Bruner outlined three modes of representation: enactive, iconic and symbolic. The essence of representation is a relationship between 'signifier' and 'signified'. In enactive representation, motor action serves as a signifier; in iconic representation, an analogue image serves as the signifier; and in symbolic representation, an arbitrary sign such as a word serves as the signifier. For each mode, according to Bruner, there are amplifiers. An amplifier is a cultural artifact that expands the range of motor, sensory, or thinking processes associated with a particular mode of representation. With his studies of the cultivation of mental skills through the symbolic forms of film, Salomon (1979) was the first to apply this notion to the audiovisual media.

Video games not only embody particular symbol systems, they do so in a context that is goal directed activity with instantaneous feedback. Activity theory, elaborated by Leont'ev (1981), emphasizes the importance of goal-directed activity in cognitive development (Gauvain 1993). The goal-directed activity involved in video games is certainly a reason for their popularity (Malone 1981) and may well be a reason for their power in exercising and stimulating cognitive skills.

Goal-directed activity has content as well as form. In principle, content and form are independent dimensions of video games, as of any other medium. In practice, however, the violent nature of much video game activity has been an ongoing cause for concern, as it has been in the older medium of television. The effects of video game violence on social behaviour have become a point of focus and needs to be researched further. The next chapter will examine this issue in more detail. One worry here is the growing availability and popularity of games featuring increasingly graphic violence.

The current chapter, however, deals with the cognitive effects of video games as interactive symbol systems and not with the social effects of their thematic content. In principle, the cognitive effects of video games are independent of any particular content. The symbolic designs are the key feature in relation to cognitive effects and similar cognitive effects should emerge regardless of thematic content, provided that presentational forms remain constant.

In practice, though, the cognitive effects of video games may not be totally independent of thematic content. Indeed, much of the research completed to date suggests that video game content and format features interact to influence game playing competency and related cognitive skill development.

Video games can be regarded as cultural artifacts that require and develop a particular set of cognitive skills; in this context they represent a cultural instrument of cognitive socialization. A major theme here is that, just as different kinds of games have, in the past, prepared children and youth for the varying adult skills required by different societies around the world (Roberts & Sutton-Smith 1962), so too do video games prepare children and youth for a future in which computer skills will become ever more crucial to thriving in a technological world.

Video games are part of a trend in cultural history that started 20,000 years ago, as the number and types of symbolic codes external to the individual mind went from none to few to many (Donald 1993). In a world in which devices for external memory storage have become increasingly important (Donald 1993), video games socialize the minds of players to deal with the symbolic systems of the computer, society's latest form of external memory storage. There was speculation early on in the history of video games that they might require and develop distinct cognitive skills (Ball 1978). Furthermore, it was theorized that video games required their own idiosyncratic literacy skills that were not the same as those normally associated with written language in print media (Greenfield 1983, 1984). Does advanced video game play depend upon a high level of development of these literacy skills? Does video game play develop specific cognitive skills that may in turn be generalizable to other forms of computer activity?

While this book is concerned with children's and teenagers' involvement with video games, evidence from young adult samples has indicated that specific cognitive skills can be learned from playing video games and these skills are transferable to other tasks. Cross-national research with American and Italian undergraduates compared the cognitive skills acquisition of experience and novice players from a video game called *Evolution* (Greenfield, Camaioni *et al.* 1994). This relatively non-violent game comprised six different levels of play, with each one introducing a new set of rules and patterns of play. Male and female players were given an opportunity to practice playing the game on their own, to do so following some initial instruction and advice on how to play, or while answering questions about their experience with the game at regular intervals during play itself. The transfer of learned skills was tested via an educational video game designed to teach the logic of computer circuitry. In this the students received a number of video demonstrations on each of which they subsequently answered questions.

Students who were already experts at playing video games performed well on the test of cognitive skill especially if they had had some opportunity to play the *Evolution* game first. Even novice players, however, benefited from playing the video game and appeared quickly to acquire essential skills which assisted them in playing with the later educational video game. Knowledge of the video game was acquired through practice and trial and error rather than by being told how to play it. The condition under which students received prior advice did not assist them to master the game. There were differences, however, between experts and novices in how effectively they responded to advice about game play strategies. Experts benefited from preplaying advice about rules and strategies of the game, while novices did not. It seems likely that experts already had well-developed schemas relevant to game playing, which enabled them to relate to and adapt the advice given to this new video game. In contrast, periodic questioning about the video game task during breaks in the initial learning procedure did help novices to acquire relevant skills and to transfer them to a subsequent task. This procedure helped in the mastery of visual aspects of the game, in particular, and this seemed to be the key to effective game play. This study is examined in more detail later in this chapter.

Early Skills Development with Computer Games

Children show the earliest signs of computer-related skills during infancy. At three years of age basic skills acquisition can become established (Strommen, Razavi and Medoff 1992). Even before then, very young infants aged between two years and three years have been observed to show an interest in a computer paintbox as an alternative to a traditional drawing and colouring set. The repertoire of early mark making exhibited with coloured felt tip pens or crayons, for example, were readily transferred to an electronic paint set (Matthews and Jessel 1993).

These basic skills reached more advanced stages of development among older children. A Japanese study showed significant developments between ages six and 12 in children's skills at playing a popular family computer game—*Super Mario Brothers*. Experienced and well-practised players performed well whether play was led with the right hand or the left hand (Kawashhima *et al.* 1991).

The conditions under which children play computer games can make a difference to performance improvement over time. One finding was that children showed greater improvements when working on a computer-based problem-solving task, couched in an adventure game format, when they played in pairs than when working at it on their own. Working in pairs not only enhanced overall performance, but also attenuated the differences normally found between girls and boys on these games. The presence of other children appears to be able to facilitate young players' computer game skills development (Littlejohn *et al.* 1992).

Spatial Skills Development and Video Games

Skill in spatial representation is one example of everyday cognitive skills utilized and developed by video games and other computer applications (Greenfield 1993). These skills build on the foundation lain down by television (Greenfield 1984; Salomon 1979). Spatial representation is better thought of as a domain of skills rather than as a single ability or skill (Pellegrino and Kail 1982). Studies to date have identified three important factors in the domain of spatial abilities: (1) spatial relations ability, which refers to the capacity to rapidly transform objects in the mind, as is required when one 'mentally rotates' an object about its centre; (2) spatial visualization, which is the ability to deal with complex visual problems that require imagining the relative movements of internal parts of a visual image, as in the folding or unfolding of flat patterns; and (3) perceptual speed, a visual-spatial factor, which involves rapid encoding and comparison of visual forms (Lohman 1979; Linn and Peterson 1985).

It is important to recognize that spatial tests assess skill in dealing with two-dimensional images of hypothetical two- or three-dimensional space. The spatial and iconic skills developed by video games are important for all sorts of computer applications from word processing (Gomez, Egan and Bowers 1986) to spreadsheets, programming, desktop publishing, databases, multimedia (Tierney *et al.* 1992), and scientific and technical simulations (Greenfield, Camaioni *et al.* 1994).

Task analyses of video games led to early speculation that they could be a tool for the development of spatial skills (Ball 1978; Greenfield 1983, 1984; Lowery and Knirk 1982-1983). This was of particular interest because of repeated findings revealing male superiority in this area. After a review of over 1000 research reports on gender differences, Maccoby and Jacklin (1974) concluded that gender differences were fairly well established in the cognitive area of spatial skills. Even when male and female performance is equal on a spatial task, there is sometimes a gender difference in strategy; males generally show preference for a more visual solution strategy whereas most females show preference for a more verbal strategy (Pezaris and Casey 1991).

Lowery and Knirk (1982-83) reasoned that if spatial skills are indeed built up over a period of time and repeated interactions, then micro-computer video games should be an excellent mechanism for training these skills. Even video games designed ostensibly for entertainment purposes may provide players with basic training in essential spatial skills. It could also be the fast-paced nature of video games that forces players to utilize spatial skills. It has been found, for example, that when given enough time, individuals tend to use a non-spatial, verbal analytical approach to problem solving or task mastery (Lohman 1979). The fast pace of video games may prevent players from using this approach and force them instead to deal with figures spatially.

Many video games do appear to involve spatial skills that go beyond simple eye-hand coordination. These spatial skills appear to be similar to the mental processes required in various spatial tests. In an article on video game playing technique, Small and Small (1982) suggested strategies for the game *Battlezone* that involved rotation in three-dimensional space. These strategies appear to be similar to the mental processes described as spatial visualization. Lowery and Knirk (1982-83) described the game *Invaders* as requiring the ability to simultaneously coordinate horizontal and vertical axes and anticipate the intersection of imaginary lines. This ability involves the same kinds of skills required to complete various tests of spatial cognitive processing.

In one of the first experimental studies utilizing video game training, Gagnon (1985) studied the effect of five hours of video game practice on undergraduate and graduate students. Subjects in the experimental group played two games (*Targ* and *Battlezone*) for two and a half hours each, whereas subjects in the control group received no video game practice. The two video games were found to utilize different, although overlapping, skills.

Gagnon reported that at the start of the study, men scored higher than women on spatial orientation, spatial visualization, and the game *Targ*, whereas women scored higher on eye-hand coordination. Following five hours of video game practice, there were no significant differences between men and women on the final scores on *Targ* and spatial visualization. However, the gender differences found at the start continued to be present on spatial orientation (in favour of men) and eye-hand coordination (in favour of women). In addition, subjects with less video game skill experience at the outset improved in spatial skills as a result of video game practice, whereas more experienced players did not. Finally, it was found that subjects who reported they had played more video games in the past tended to score higher on both the video games and the spatial tests. Thus, both gender and amount of past video game practice were related to subjects' scores on video games and spatial skills.

Although Gagnon (1985) did not obtain overall differences between experimental subjects and control subjects on paper-and-pencil Spatial Visualization, Spatial Orientation, and Visual Pursuit tests, post hoc analyses indicated that women in the experimental group showed more improvement on the Spatial Visualization post-test than women in the control group. There were no differences among men on any test. Gagnon suggested that because the women did not perform as well as the men initially on all of the pretests, they might have been able to benefit from playing the video games whereas men did not do so.

Because the five hours of video game practice all occurred within a one week period and this practice time was equally split between two different games, it is possible that subjects did not have enough time to gain much expertise in these video games. Alternatively, Gagnon may have found limited gains in spatial skill performance after playing *Targ* and *Battlezone* because the measures of spatial skill were static, paper-and-pencil measures of the skills and consequently different from the utilization of those skills during video game play.

In another set of practice studies, Pepin and Dorval (1986) and Dorval and Pepin (1986) provided eight sessions of training on the video game *Zaxxon* (each session included five games of *Zaxxon*) to 70 undergraduate students in Quebec city. Training was also provided to 101 seventh-grade students in Quebec city, although the children received fewer practice sessions because of time constraints. A control group was given only the pretest and post-test and received no training. Scores on the Space Relations Test of the Differential Aptitude Test (DAT), Forms A and B, were used as measures of spatial ability.

In the adult experiment, there were no significant gender-related differences in visual-spatial skills, although there was a tendency toward a difference in favour of men. Furthermore, both men and women gained significantly and equally on the spatial measures from playing *Zaxxon*. In the experiment with adolescents, there was no initial gender difference in visual-spatial skills and no significant improvement in spatial skills following training on *Zaxxon*. One possible reason that adults but not adolescents, improved is that the adult sample had no prior experience with video games, whereas the adolescent sample had some experience, although it was very limited.

Others have found stronger support for the hypothesis that video game playing can improve spatial skill performance (e.g. Forsyth and Lancy 1987; McClurg and Chaille 1987; Subrahmanyam and Greenfield 1994). For example, McClurg and Chaille (1987) reported that playing computer games enhanced the development of the spatial skill of three-dimensional mental rotation in fifth-, seventh-, and ninth-grade students (ages 10-11, 12-13, 15-16 years respectively), with the treatment benefiting both boys and girls at all three grade levels equally. It is interesting to note, that in their study, there was an initial gender difference in spatial skill, with boys performing better than the girls; it is not clear from their article whether this difference continued to be present at the end of the study. Miller and Kapel (1985) found a positive effect of similar computer games on two-dimensional mental rotation in seventh and eighth graders.

Thus, there is evidence that in some age groups, with some games, video games are a tool of cognitive socialization for some skills of spatial representation. There is also evidence that these games can reduce some gender differences in the spatial skills of adults. Subrahmanyam and Greenfield (1994) investigated the question of whether this effect could be obtained in a stronger form if video game practice was given to children at crucial points in their cognitive development. They conducted research into the impact of video game practice among ten-year-olds. Their study was carried out with the game *Marble Madness* which involves guiding a marble along a three-dimensional grid using a joystick. In this game, players have to be careful to keep the marble on a path and try and prevent it from falling off, while avoiding small worm-like creatures that cause the marble to disappear temporarily on contact. The game has increasing levels of difficulty. At lower levels, players have to simply trace a given path, taking care to prevent the marble from falling off and to avoid the black ball and the worm-like creatures. At higher levels, the grid becomes more complex and even involves a maze in the final level. At all levels, the players have to reach the end point of one level within the time allotted before they can move on to start again at the first level. If players are unsuccessful at a given level, they have to start again at the first level and work their way up.

This particular game was chosen because it involves the use of the spatial skills of guiding objects, judging speeds and distances of moving objects, and intercepting objects. In addition, it was also found to be a challenging game that children enjoyed playing. Another computer game, *Conjecture*, was used as a control condition in the study. This is a word game and does not involve any spatial skills. It involves solving puzzles in which, using some initial cues, the player has to fill in blanks in words that stand for phrases, capitals, and things.

Spatial abilities were measured using a computer-based test battery (Pellegrino *et al.* 1987). Three different tests were used called Memory Lane, Extrapolation, and Intercept. In Memory Lane, each subject was presented with three sequential displays consisting of three small squares moving across the screen. Of these three paths, either the first or the third was different from the second. The subject had to judge which of the paths (either the first or the third) was different from the second one. In Extrapolation, the subject had to extrapolate mentally the location of a trajectory (straight, sine, or parabola) and then use a joystick to move an arrow to the point where he or she estimated the line would end. In Intercept, the subject had to press the space bar of the keyboard to trigger a missile in order to intercept a UFO that was released. The UFO would trace a path that was either a straight line, a sine curve, or a parabola.

The results showed that video game practice, but not practice on a computerized word game, led to significant improvement in dynamic spatial skills, an improvement that was concentrated in those subjects who started out with relatively poor spatial performance. According to Subrahmanyam and Greenfield, video game practice could therefore serve as compensatory education for relatively weak spatial skills.

The ability to learn a video game was strongly related to spatial skill. Initial spatial skill significantly predicted ultimate attainment on *Marble Madness*. However, it did not predict initial levels of performance. One possible reason for there being no relation between spatial skill and initial performance on *Marble Madness* could be that the index of game performance was not very sensitive to differences at the beginning, when almost all subjects failed on the first level, leading to a nonsignificant result.

No evidence emerged from this study that past history of video game playing made any difference to performance in the video game the children had to learn to play. This may have been due to a lack of sensitivity in the measure of previous game playing behaviour which involved a rather global indicator of playing and failed to distinguish between past playing of video games that did or did not involve the spatial skills required by the current video game.

Video game practice tended to equalize spatial performance among groups, but it had the opposite effect on video game performance. In the experimental group, there were no gender differences in initial scores on *Marble Madness*; but after several hours of practice, boys showed significantly better performance than girls did. Thus, the same amount of video game practice led to lesser improvement in game skill for girls. One factor may be that because of boys' greater previous video game experience, they 'learned how to learn' a new video game better than girls.

Other research on video game training obtained mild, mixed or no effects of training among older respondents (Dorval and Pepin 1986; Gagnon 1985). Even research conducted by Greenfield and her colleagues found that the strong training effects found among ten-year-olds did not emerge as readily among older children (Greenfield, Brannon and Lohr 1994; Greenfield, Camaioni *et al.* 1994).

Okagaki and Frensch (1994) conducted a replication of Subrahmanyam and Greenfield's study with an older sample of video game players. They also studied the effect of video game play on the specific component of spatial skills utilized in the game. Thus, if a video game relied heavily on two spatial skills, was the impact on those skills predictable? In this study, adolescents in their late teens played a video game called *Tetris*. Afterwards, the players were given four paper-and-pencil tests assessing mental rotation, spatial visualization, and perceptual speed. The game required the rapid rotation and placement of seven different-shaped blocks. These shapes must be placed in holes in a wall so that no holes remain. Players are timed in their ability to make accurate placements of shapes to holes. In some instances, the shapes have to be rotated to fit in their proper place.

In a second experiment, the aims were essentially the same, with the difference that computerized rather than paper-and-pencil measures of mental rotation and spatial visualization were used. The results showed throughout that playing *Tetris* improved performance on these tasks. In general, males fared better than females on these tasks. In paper-and-pencil tests, male performance improved while female did not. On the computerized tests, both males and females exhibited some improvement in task abilities.

The importance of this study was the finding that there were gains in spatial performance as a function of playing a popular video game and after only six hours of playing practice. The implication of this is that adolescent video game players can accrue some specific cognitive benefits from the time they spend playing video games.

Spatial skills closely related to those applied in playing the video game benefited most. Both male and female players exhibited improvements in these skills. The idea fostered by Subrahmanyam and Greenfield (1994) that there may be a particularly sensitive period, up to age ten or 12, when spatial skills show the greatest development, was not supported by Okagaki and Frensch, whose findings indicated that similarity between the video game and spatial skills task was the key factor. If the degree of similarity here was great enough, transfer of skills from the video game to a different task would occur even among players in their mid-teens. There was even some generalization of learning from the video game to tasks that required slightly modified spatial skills. Playing *Tetris*, for example, enhanced players' abilities to place both *Tetris*-type shapes and non-*Tetris*-type shapes into their appropriate slots.

Cognitive Skills and Action Video Games

A number of researchers have investigated the kinds of cognitive skills needed to play arcade-type video games with action themes. Craig (1987) found that the progression from novice to expert in the course of mastering *Passport to Paris*, an action game requiring logical problem-solving, involved developing systematic organization, sensitivity to efficient use of constrained resources (time, money), and evaluation and revision. Age is an important factor in relation to the mastery of action video games. Research has shown, for instance, that players aged 12 and 20 improved with practice in their performance on a video game called *Asteroids*, whereas children aged four to seven years did not (Roberts *et al.* 1991). Expert video game players use anticipatory eye movements to calibrate future action (Roberts and Ondrejko 1995).

Lancy and his colleagues experimented with the cognitive aspects of two non-action genres of computers—fantasy adventure games and interactive fiction—as well as with the cognitive aspects of action video games (Forsyth and Lancy 1987; Hayes, Lancy and Evans 1985; Lancy 1987; Lancy *et al.* 1985; Lancy and Hayes 1988). An adventure game, *Winnie the Pooh*, led to the acquisition of game-related spatial knowledge (Forsyth 1986; Forsyth and Lancy 1987), whereas interactive fiction, requiring a great deal of reading, was enjoyed by reluctant readers (Lancy 1987; Lancy and Hayes 1988).

More recent research conducted with students in their late teens has provided further evidence that commercially-developed video games designed to provide home entertainment can be adapted to test the development and implementation of certain cognitive skills. This work, conducted by Greenfield and her colleagues, has indicated that video games do exercise specific categories of cognitive skill.

One experiment conducted in the United States and Italy, which was introduced earlier in this chapter, examined computer games as cultural tools of cognitive socialization. It also investigated the cognitive processes involved in mastering computer games (Greenfield, Camaioni *et al.* 1994). Exposure to computer technology, either in the long term through the natural experience of playing these games, or in the short term via the use of these games as part of this experiment, was associated with greater skill in understanding and interpreting scientific and technical information presented graphically on a computer screen. It was linked in particular with a growing preference for assimilating information through pictures rather than words.

Groups of undergraduate students in Los Angeles and Rome took part in the study. The participants were initially distinguished as experienced or novice computer game players. Not surprisingly, males were found to be more experienced with these games than were females. The students played over three sessions with a nonviolent game called *Evolution*. In one condition, they simply practised playing the game. In a second condition, they were given a lecture about the game and a video demonstration of an expert playing it. In a third condition, they completed written answers to questions about the game and their experience of it. In Rome, two further conditions were added. In one, students played a computer memory game, and in the second, they played a mechanical memory game that presented the same task as the video game in mechanical form. The transfer of learned skills was tested via an educational video game designed to teach the logic of computer circuitry. In this, the students received a number of video demonstrations on each of which they subsequently answered questions.

Knowledge of a video game was acquired as a result of the inductive experience of playing the game. There was a significant and steady increase in knowledge of rules, regularities and strategies as a function of time spent playing the video game *Evolution*. The study also established that the provision of initial information through slides, verbal instructions, and modelling did not make a difference in the ultimate game skill attained by students. Thus, it was necessary for players to form hypotheses from their own experience and to test them inductively in the course of the game. A model and explanations that could aid deductive processes at the outset of the learning process were of no advantage for either novices or more experienced players.

Greenfield, Camaioni *et al.* (1994) established that inductive discovery is crucial to mastery of an arcade-style action video game. Harris (1992) cited by Greenfield and her colleagues reportedly found that with children, novices are introduced to game play by more experienced players who explain the basics of the game to newcomers, following which they develop their own strategies. Elsewhere, researchers have found that instructions about play introduced after some initial practice can help a new player to master a video game (Newell *et al.* 1989).

Greenfield, Camaioni *et al.* (1994) pointed to key differences between the procedures adopted by these other researchers and their own study in explaining differences in their respective results. In the Harris study, expert instructions were apparently fed to the novice players while they were on-line with the game. Thus, the creation of personal play models occurred simultaneously with reception of instructions from elsewhere. With Newell *et al.* (1989), their findings showed that instructions before playing (as in Greenfield's study) were less effective than instructions given afterwards.

Experts and novices differed, however, in how effectively they responded to advice about game play strategies. Experts benefited from preplaying communication about the rules and strategies of the game, while novices did not. It seems likely, though, that experts had already developed relevant game playing schemas that they were able to adapt in the light of preplaying advice for a new game.

Periodic questioning about the task during breaks in the initial learning procedure did help novices to transfer more effectively the skills acquired during training to the actual game itself. This procedure assisted the mastery of iconic or visual aspects of the game, which seemed to be the key to effective game play. This was further underlined by the finding that prior practice with an iconically similar computer training system was particularly helpful to gaining effective video game-related skills.

Greenfield, Brannon and Lohr (1994) tested whether video games could contribute to the development of spatial representational skills required for humans to 'interface' effectively with computer technology, an increasingly important part of the ecology of modern society. American undergraduate students took part in a study that examined the relationship between skill levels in playing a three-dimensional action arcade video game, *The Empire Strikes Back* and the skills needed to complete a mental paper-folding task.

In *The Empire Strikes Back*, the game gives the player the perspective of a starship pilot flying through space. The player's task is to shoot enemy ships while avoiding asteroids and enemy fire so as to accumulate points and advance in difficulty level. The game requires players to navigate through three-dimensional space, represented on a two-dimensional screen. The test of visual spatial skills, mental paper folding, was also one that demanded visualizing three-dimensional movement from a two-dimensional display. The key difference between the video game and paper folding test was that the former was dynamic, involving a lot of movement, while the latter was static.

Performance in playing the video game was correlated with ability to complete the mental paper folding task in one study. In a second study, there was no short-term effect of playing the video game on mental paper folding ability, but some evidence did emerge that in the longer-term, video game expertise could be beneficial to this kind of task. Practice was needed over an extended period of time to cultivate these skills.

With the rapid growth in penetration of video games during the late 1970s and throughout the 1980s, a number of anxieties surfaced concerning the possibly harmful side-effects regular playing of these games might have on children and teenagers. Of particular concern in this respect were some suggested adverse effects upon the development of literacy and related intellectual abilities.

As the way in which the games are played has been examined more closely, however, it has become apparent that they involve a range of cognitive skills, which can become very acutely developed in individuals who are well-practised in video game play. Video games are not simply an appealing pastime for young people, they may serve as an introduction to the world of computers. Furthermore, they have been found to cultivate certain categories of cognitive skill that are important in the context of other types of computer use. Indeed, some of the mental and information processing skills acquired through playing video games may be transferable to other domains of experience. Far from impeding the intellectual growth of young people, video games may be able to stimulate it. Although, excessive video game play, to the neglect of other pursuits—mental or physical—is not a habit that should be encouraged, there do, nevertheless, seem to be some positive and beneficial side-effects to young people's involvement with these games, which need to be more fully elaborated, understood and cultivated. In a world that is increasingly run by computers, it is becoming ever more important that we become a computer literate society. Video games may have a significant part to play in achieving this objective.

Chapter Five

Effects of
Video Games on Social Behaviour

Over the past two decades a significant body of research has been gathered that indicates that viewing television violence can have potentially harmful effects on children (Friedrich-Cofer and Huston 1986; Gauntlett 1995). Televized depictions of violence can allegedly teach children to use violence themselves under different circumstances, provide justification for doing so, and render them less concerned about the hurt or suffering violence can cause to victims. It has also been contended that children who observe aggressive television models sometimes imitate those behaviours or have disinhibited the internal controls that prevent aggressive action (Stein and Friedrich 1972; Steuer, Applefield and Smith 1971). Blood pressure increases after viewing sexual or aggressive content provide physiological support for the arousal theory that purports that such material can cause viewers to become emotionally aroused in a non-specific way, creating a predisposition for aggression under appropriate environmental circumstances (Zillmann 1971). However, children rarely act less aggressively after viewing televized violence as would be predicted by a drive-reduction hypothesis (Friedrich-Cofer and Huston 1986).

Extrapolating from the work done with television, a variety of undesirable effects might be hypothesized to follow from playing computer or video games with violent themes, such as the heightening of perceptions of personal risk or danger in the real world, decreasing concern for the victims of violence, weakening of social conditioned inhibitions against behaving aggressively, and the adoption of imitable violent role models with whom players have interacted in these games (Funk and Buckman 1995).

In contrast to the above concerns, some writers have suggested that viewing media violence can have more positive benefits. According to the notion of catharsis, becoming involved with media portrayals of violence can facilitate the discharge of aggressive impulses (Feshbach and Singer 1971). Another view is that through exposure to media violence that depicts the victim's suffering, positive lessons can be learned about the harms caused by violence leading children to re-think their own use of aggressiveness (Kunkel *et al.* 1996).

Many video games have violent themes and therefore often require aggressive performance by participants (Dominick 1984; Loftus and Loftus 1983). In many video games, players must shoot or harm their symbolic opponents in order to win. Violence is, in fact, a theme which pervades many of the most popular games. One of the most successful Nintendo games in recent years, *Streetfighter* II, centres around a kick-boxing tournament. Variations on this central theme occur in the form of the different locations in the world where the tournament is staged. These include a Brazilian dock, an Indian temple, a Chinese street market, a Soviet factory and a Las Vegas show palace. In the Indian setting, elephants are shown swaying their trunks in the background, while in a Spanish setting, flamenco dancers perform and crowds cheer as the combatants battle for supremacy. Even those games that pride themselves on stretching players intellectually have sometimes had violent features added to allay distributors' anxieties about games being able to compete on the basis of their purported educational benefits alone. *Sim City* (described in Chapter Four) is a simulation that allows players to design their own city. But even this challenging game had features such as earthquakes, nuclear meltdowns and even an attack from Godzilla added to alleviate distributors' concerns that the game would be seen as 'too educational'. Some critics have argued that these disaster features are unnecessary (Barol 1989).

There is little doubt that video games with violent themes have been extremely popular with youngsters. Provenzo (1991) analyzed Nintendo's ten most popular games and found that they all contained violence. In eight cases, violence, in the form of martial arts, was the central theme. The other two cases comprised adventure games with elements of violence. The key elements of the storyline in these games comprised rescue, revenge and the battle of good versus evil. The rescuer was usually male and the victim being rescued was generally female. A crucial factor linked to how the child might react to the violence in these games was whether or not there was some scope for distinguishing clearly between good and bad. The significance of this point is that the child might be less likely to experience raised aggressive impulses as a function of playing a game with a violent theme, if the violence was used purposefully and with justification in the resolution of a fantasy storyline through which a child could vicariously discharge any personal feelings of aggression. The problem with this hypothetical outcome is that it would be dependent on the game having sufficiently well-developed characterizations and plot to facilitate the necessary degree of psychological involvement.

Consistent with television studies on observed aggression, research has begun to suggest that children who play aggressive video games may subsequently become more aggressive in their social play. If this observation is true, then there is good reason for concern given the prevalence of video games with violent themes.

One estimate calculated that around 70 per cent of all the video games licensed by Nintendo. one of the market leaders, had violent action levels high enough to be harmful to children (Wood 1990). Following widespread public debate about the possible ills of video games with violent themes, the leading manufacturers began, in the early 1990s, to introduce their own codes of practice and ratings systems. Nintendo attempted to maintain strict rules about the types of violence to be included in their games, with prohibitions placed on graphic violence and the presence of blood. Sega developed a self-imposed rating system for its games, although critics condemned this system as a ploy to continue producing games with violence and sex (Brandt, Gross and Coy 1994). Games in this manufacturer's *Mortal Kombat* series were illustrative of a new brand of violent video game themes. Real provides a cogent description of these games. In the first issue of *Mortal Kombat*, a greater photographic visual realism was combined with graphic violence:

> A solid punch sends animated blood flying, a loser knocked off a ledge lands impaled on a spike, a still-pulsing heart is ripped out by hand, and an opponent's head is torn off and held up victoriously with the spinal cord dangling from its neck ... The sequel *Mortal Kombat* II, countered the violence with clever twists. When warrior Kitana punches deadly Shang Tsung, gooey blood spills out; when she throws razor-edged fans, more blood splatters ... (1996: 84).

Playing video and computer games has become a valued leisure activity among children and adolescents, who often prefer violent games. One survey carried out in the United States found that between eight and nine out of ten video games examined involved participants in acts of simulated destruction, killing or violence (Bowman and Rotter 1983). A more recent observation, again from the United States, indicated that by 1990 one in three American homes had video games, with children in those homes playing up to 40 hours a week, and with roughly 80 per cent of the games containing violence (Milloy 1991). What specific impact, then, does video game violence have upon the young people who play these games?

There are good reasons to believe that some of the psychological mechanisms believed to underpin effects television allegedly can have upon young viewers, such as imitative modelling and the giving rise to ideas about violence and strategies for its successful deployment, could also play a role in the shaping of behaviour by video games. Two additional factors may be important during video game playing, however, which have been referred to as participant modelling and reward reinforcement.

Video games involve a type of participant modelling in that the player who controls an on-screen character in the course of playing a video game in some ways becomes that character. For example, when playing Pac-man, which for many of the early years was the most popular video game on the market, the player is put into the position of controlling a creature that flees from four monsters and at times destroys those monsters. Furthermore, the player is rewarded for performing these behaviours effectively; the more adept the player is at escaping the monsters and destroying them, the more points he or she receives and the longer the game lasts.

Research has yet to reveal much about the longer-term impact of playing violent video games. Public concern about their effects has nevertheless arisen because such games engage the active involvement of children who can participate directly in and manipulate events that occur on screen. In contrast, when watching television, viewers are passive receivers of a one-way flow of communication (Bowman and Rotter 1983). The power of video or computer games may also derive from the feeling of control which they stimulate in young players (Greenfield 1984).

Electronic game research has usually followed strategies from research evaluating the effects of television (Dominick 1984; Funk 1992;

Selnow 1984). As with television, playing video games provides opportunities for observational learning. In addition to the relatively passive influence of watching television, playing electronic games adds an active dimension that may intensify the impact of game playing (Chambers and Ascione 1987). Most games require the player to take part in developing the game scenario, but players are routinely rewarded for identifying and selecting the strategies built in by the game designer.

In violent games, the game ends with the player's defeat or obliteration if he or she fails to choose the predetermined strategy. These games typically offer no options for compromise and often reinforce negative stereotypes, particularly a pervasive view of women as brainless victims (Provenzo 1991). The antisocial behaviour often required to win rarely generates realistic consequences, and the true impact of violent actions is obscured.

As yet there is insufficient research to support strong causal statements about the impact of playing violent electronic games. Some findings suggest that gender of player, time spent, and location of play (home or arcade) are key predictor variables. There are also some intriguing trends consistent with the results of parallel television research. The research done so far indicates that video game effects upon children's and adolescents' behavioural tendencies may operate through many of the same psychological mechanisms invoked to explain the alleged effects of television violence. These include imitation, disinhibition and arousal.

In assessing the types of effects computer or video games can have, researchers have, thus far, deployed a variety of research methodologies. Some researchers have surveyed young people to collect their personal reactions to such games, others have observed the way they play, while others have manipulated the circumstances under which video game play takes place.

Personal Reactions to Video Game Effects

Computer and video games offer young people a unique environment in which to enjoy themselves, engage with an attractive high-tech medium which, in some instances, has a certain cache because of military connections. Video game playing in arcades also represents a social environment that is off-limits to parents and other adults and provides a means to establish a distinct sub-culture among same-age peers with the same interests. According to Provenzo:

> Video game arcades, and to a lesser extent home video game systems, provide their users with an alternative social and cultural space ... In addition, video games ... provide extremely powerful symbols that can be used to mold a youth subculture (1991: 58).

Young people have been surveyed and interviewed about their use of computer or video games and asked to provide self-reports of how much they believe they are affected by these games. On some occasions, evidence has been obtained not only from children themselves, but also from their parents and teachers.

The research evidence that derives from this approach has not always been consistent. One early survey found that video game playing was apparently correlated with aggressive tendencies on the subject. This study questioned both girls and boys, aged 15 to 16 years, about their playing of video games in arcades and at home, and obtained from them some indication of how often they reacted aggressively in certain situations. Three types of aggression measure were used. The first of these required the teenage respondents to indicate how they would respond—aggressively or non-aggressively—in a number of hypothetical scenarios. The second measure attempted to ascertain young respondents' attitudes towards the use of physical aggression more generally. The third measure assessed delinquent tendencies among the teenage sample.

The playing of arcade video games was linked with watching violent programmes on television. Both boys and girls who watched more television violence tended to spend more time and more money playing these arcade games. The playing of video games at home was also linked to watching violence on television, but primarily for boys. Reported frequency of playing arcade video games was found initially to be significantly correlated with each of the three measures of aggression. In each case, however, when other factors such as school performance level and television violence viewing were controlled, these correlations disappeared (Dominick 1984). Elsewhere, video game playing was found to exhibit some degree of association with the attitudes 11- to 16-year-old boys held about war (Rushbrook 1986).

Another survey of children and teenagers, aged between 12 and 14 years, in Canada found little evidence to indicate that going to video arcades was closely connected with delinquency. There was hardly anything to suggest that video arcades facilitated deviant behaviour among teenagers. The only tentative connection derived from a finding that among the older children surveyed, those who regularly went to video arcades tended to stay out later at night. In turn, those who stayed out late were somewhat more likely to be involved in delinquent behaviour (Ellis 1984). This research was corroborated further in Australia where a survey of 11- to 16-year-olds produced no evidence that video game playing was directly linked to adolescent delinquency (Abbott, Palmisano and Dickerson 1995).

With slightly older video game players who had gone to college, levels of propensity to hostility after playing with violent video games, as measured by a standardized test, were found to be correlated with the *extent* of playing such games (Anderson and Ford 1986). This result was confirmed elsewhere (Mehrabian and Wixen 1986). As the amount of video game playing increases, so too does the likelihood that children themselves will report acting more aggressively (Fling *et al.* 1992).

Teachers have also indicated that boys, aged ten to 12 years, with whom they have had regular contact in school, have been observably more impulsive and aggressive in their behaviour if they were known to be regular video game players (Linn and Lepper 1987). Not all researchers have found this sort of relationship. One study of individuals aged 12 to 34 years found no link between the amount of video game play in which they indulged and measures of hostility or self-esteem (Gibb *et al.* 1983). Another study found that video games could even have a calming effect on teenagers aged 11 to 14 years (Kestenbaum and Weinstein 1985).

In Britain, a survey of video game playing adolescents asked them if they thought that playing violent video games made them more aggressive. Apparently, they did feel that they experienced this kind of effect (Griffiths and Hunt 1993). Furthermore, the more frequently they played, the more they felt they were influenced in this way. There is, of course, more than one way of interpreting these results. Aggressive children could be drawn to video games rather than their aggression resulting from the playing of such games. With self-report studies, the correlational evidence is not always convincing. Basic correlational relationships may reveal little about causal connections between playing computer or video games and how children or young people behave.

There may be other factors, which often remain unmeasured, which underpin both propensity to play video games and propensity to behave aggressively.

Experimental Research into Video Game Playing

One way of dealing with the issue of causation, which surveys frequently have problems with, is to set up circumstances under which the conditions of video game playing are systematically manipulated and in which different features are controlled by the researcher. With this approach, children and young people play selected video games with particular characteristics and their amount of playing as well as the type of game played are controlled by the experimenter.

Some researchers have observed that young children become demonstrably more aggressive after exposure to violent video games (Funk 1992; Griffiths 1991b). Results have been less consistent and clear cut with older children (Funk and Buckman 1995, 1996)

Imitation and Instigation

There are different ways in which the effects of video games can be investigated in this controlled fashion. As with experimental research on the effects of televized violence, children can be tested for their propensity to imitate the things they see on screen, or their general tendencies to behave more aggressively, whether or not their behaviour resembles anything just seen on screen. Some researchers have relied not simply on overt behavioural measures; these are sometimes supplemented by measures of physiological arousal. These different kinds of effects measures have been deployed in research on the impact of video games.

One classic type of experiment on the effects of television violence carried out with children involves observing children at play before and after they have been given an opportunity to watch an excerpt from a movie or television programme. Under different conditions, the excerpts chosen may contain violence or non-violent material. This design has been applied, in a small number of studies, to the investigation of effects of video game violence on children.

Cooper and Mackie (1986) looked for changes in the play behaviour of ten-year-old children before and after playing video games that had either violent or non-violent themes. In fact, the children studied were assigned to pairs in which one child played a video game while the other child watched. The latter child was given no opportunity to play. This approach was designed to find out if actively engaging with a video game produced different kinds of reactions among children than did passively watching another child play. All the children were observed playing in a room full of toys before and after they engaged with the video game.

In this study, there was little difference in patterns of behaviour between players and watchers, but the type of video game with which the child engaged did make a difference to the way some of the children behaved. The impact of violence in a video game was found to have an effect on how children played, but curiously this effect was largely confined to girls. Those girls who played with a violent video game subsequently exhibited more general activity and more aggressive behaviour in a free play situation. Girls who had themselves played with or watched another individual play with a violent video game also showed more interest subsequently in playing with an aggressive toy. In contrast, after playing a non-violent video game, the girls' behaviour became quieter. No such effects were observed among the boys in the sample. Boys' behaviour showed no major changes as a result of video game playing. Boys had a stronger tendency to choose to play with aggressive toys than did girls anyway, but this propensity was not altered by playing with a violent video game. The researchers suggested that girls may have reacted to the violent nature of the violent video game more so than did boys because they were less used to being exposed to violence on screen in this way. Girls may have felt freer to play more aggressively after being encouraged to play a video game with a strong violent theme.

A later study used a similar research design to investigate the impact of violence in video games upon the play behaviour of even younger children, aged five to seven years (Schutte *et al.* 1988). Here boys and girls were allocated randomly to play with either a violent video game (based on martial arts movements) or a non-violent video game (jungle vine swinging), and were then observed while playing.

The violent video game used in this study was called *Karateka* and involved a protagonist who was supposed to hit or kick villains enough to kill them and ultimately to save a damsel in distress. The villain could kill the protagonist by striking him more often than he was struck by the protagonist. The non-violent game was called *Jungle Hunt* and involved a protagonist who was supposed to jump from one swinging vine to another. The task was to have the character jump at the right time so as to avoid falling and perishing.

The findings indicated that young children who had played the video game with the more violent theme were subsequently more likely to show aggressive tendencies during a following free play situation. It is perhaps worth remarking, however, that the study used only one violent video game. This raises a question of whether it was specifically the violence in *Karateka* which set the children off at play, or some other feature in the game which excited them. The fact that the children tended to be more likely to exhibit play behaviours similar to those depicted in the game suggested that video games could shape behaviour after its own form, if opportunities for copying those behaviours were presented to the children. Children who played the jungle swinging game, for example, were more likely to play with the jungle swing in the play room. Those youngsters who had played *Karateka* displayed more subsequent hitting and kicking behaviour aimed both at the toys in the room and at other children in there with them.

Elsewhere, contradictory evidence on the effect of violent video games has emerged. Older children, in their mid-teens showed no increase in aggressiveness towards same-age individuals, after playing a video game with a violent theme, in a simulated situation prepared by the researchers in which the players were given opportunities to behave in a hostile way. There was no evidence, in the short term at least, that teenagers would imitate the violence in video games (Winkel, Novak and Hopson 1987).

Arousal Effects

One factor thought to mediate the effects of televized violence is the capacity of such media content to produce physiological arousal in viewers. Arousal serves to enhance the likelihood of a behavioural response. The nature of the latter is significantly influenced by environmental cues and may take the form of aggression should a situation warrant that type of reaction from the individual. A number of studies have begun to explore the capability of video games to arouse players emotionally and physiologically, thus opening up an increased possibility of subsequent aggressive responding.

Winkel, Novak and Hopson (1984) examined the relationships among personality factors, physiological arousal and aggression after playing video games among individuals in their early adolescence. The effects of the aggressive content of the games on subsequent aggression was also assessed. The two independent variables consisted of gender of player and video game content (very aggressive vs. aggressive vs. non-aggressive). The dependent measures included participants' responses to a personality inventory, physiological arousal (heart rate), and aggressive behaviour. Winkel, Novak and Hopson found that the content of the video game (i.e. aggressive vs. non-aggressive) did not affect the subsequent behaviour of the user. Furthermore, the aggressive nature of the video games employed in the investigation did not lead to increased physiological arousal.

Lynch (1994) hypothesized that playing video games with violent content would produce greater cardiovascular responses in adolescent males than those playing non-violent games. This study examined heart rate and blood pressure differences between 76 subjects (aged 12 to 16 years) who played either violent or non-violent games, but found no differences between the two groups.

A further study of college students examined the impact of playing or observing a violent virtual reality game (Calvert and Tan 1994). In virtual reality, and in many CD-ROM format games, various special effects and peripheral equipment give the player a heightened sense of involvement, even immersion, in the game (Biocca 1994). Some propose that this perceptual absorption will increase the impact of game playing (Patkin 1994).

In the Calvert and Tan (1994) study, 36 college students (half of whom were female) either played, observed, or were led through the motions typical of the violent game. Those who played the violent virtual reality game demonstrated subsequent increases in physiological responses and aggressive thoughts, compared to observers and simulation participants. These results suggest that increasing the realism of violent electronic games may increase the influence of game content.

Reducing Prosocial Behaviour

Video games may have effects on young people other than ones linked to violent behaviour. One experimental study examined the impact of video games with violent or prosocial themes upon children's subsequent giving behaviour (Chambers and Ascione 1987). The prosocial theme game was the *Smurfs* by Coleco. In this game, a character attempts to rescue another character after avoiding a series of hazards. The violent theme game was *Boxing* by Atari in which two players each control a 'boxer' character. Each boxer character tries to hit the other.

All the children, aged between eight and 14 years, were given US $1.00 in five cents pieces and left alone in a room with a donation box. Here, they were given the opportunity to put as many nickels (if any) as they liked in the box. A second measure of helping behaviour was assessed by leaving each child alone in a room for five minutes with a choice between sharpening pencils for the experimenter or reading some books. The amount of each donation served as the measure of giving and the number of pencils sharpened was a measure of helping behaviour. The scores on these two measures provided an indication of the strength of impact of a particular type (violent or prosocial) of video game.

Prior to the donating and helping opportunities, the children played either a violent video game or one with a prosocial theme. They played either on their own or cooperatively with another child. The results showed that children were less likely to give money to a donation box after playing a violent video game than one with a prosocial theme. Playing the prosocial video game did not increase the amount of helping or giving behaviour, but playing a violent video game acted to reduce these behaviours.

Even with experimental studies, there are problems of validity that derive from the fact that they do not measure 'real aggression' but rather simulated or pretend aggression. One writer has argued that studies that report changes in these measures of fantasy aggression following video game play actually provide support for the catharsis hypothesis, rather than the aggression stimulation effects violent video games are widely believed to have. The increased production of fantasy hostile energy in pretend aggressive situations may represent and measure a discharge of hostility through the vicarious experiences engendered by these games rather than an increase in real aggression (Griffiths 1996).

Observing Video Game Play

Another way of investigating the impact of violent video games on young people's social attitudes and behaviour is to observe them while playing such games and then again afterwards. With children, in particular, it is possible to observe them at play after they have been playing with games that have violent or other themes. Very often, these studies adopt an experimental paradigm in which video game exposure or subsequent play conditions are manipulated in advance by the researcher. In one example of this kind of study, Cooper and Mackie (1986) observed the free play of nine- and ten-year-old children in a room full of toys after they had played or watched other children playing video games. The interesting results that emerged from this study were that girls were seen to become more aggressive at play, while boys were unaffected. Whether the children played the games themselves or watched while other children played, made no difference to the pattern of play behaviour that followed.

Silvern and Williamson (1987) observed young children in a free play situation after they had been shown a violent cartoon or played *Invaders*. Children's behaviour was coded according to a framework devised by Greer et al. (1982). This coding frame is shown below.

A. *Aggression*

1. Physical aggression—physical attack, obstruction, teasing, threatening gestures.
2. Verbal aggression—angry commands, verbal teasing, derogation.
3. Object aggression—physical attack on an object.

B. *Imaginative fantasy*

1. Solitary fantasy—storytelling alone and/or acting out a fantasy role.
2. Collaborative fantasy—both children are storytelling and/or acting out fantasy roles whole involved in social interaction.
3. Fantasy aggression—aggression as part of fantasy, for example, pretending to have a ray gun battle while playing a space hero.

C. *Positive social interaction*

1. Verbal interaction—verbalization/vocalization to other child

(includes laughing, storytelling, and other non-aggressive verbal/ vocal communication to other child).

The results indicated that a violent video game and a violent cartoon both raised levels of aggression in young children relative to a baseline condition. This finding supported earlier results (Favaro 1984) in which adults indicated that aggressive experiences seemed to increase levels of aggression.

The increased aggression found in this study was explained in terms of social learning theory and arousal theory. Social learning theory (that children model behaviour that they observe) might be a plausible explanation in regard to increased aggression as a result of watching the cartoon. Even though the cartoon was an animation, the characters of *Roadrunner* and *Wily Coyote* had many human attributes (such as voice, personality and understandable motivation). These may have been sufficient to invoke a degree of identification with these characters and their behaviours which, in turn, mediated the post-viewing aggressive responding of very young viewers.

The social learning type of explanation was regarded as less tenable in relation to the video game. *Invaders* was seen to be so abstract in nature that it would be unlikely to provide characters with whom young children might identify. An alternative hypothesis is that video games such as *Invaders* are arousing. During game playing the sympathetic nervous system reacts at an instinctual level so that the player begins to feel a nonspecific but aroused emotional effect, which increases the likelihood of children demonstrating those behaviours that were most recently observed or experienced.

These increases in aggression observed by Silvern and Williamson (1987) were similar to those that followed watching violent cartoons. In a study of 31 five and seven-year-olds, children tended to imitate the behaviour of main characters from previously played video games, whether aggressive or non-aggressive (Schutte *et al.* 1988). Researchers have noted increases in the activity level and aggressive free play of 40 fifth-grade girls after playing or just observing another aggressive video game (Cooper and Mackie 1986).

Recently, Irwin and Gross (1995) measured interpersonal aggression and aggression toward inanimate objects in 60 boys aged seven and eight years. After playing video games with aggressive and non-aggressive themes, they found that those boys who played the aggressive-theme games exhibited significantly more object aggression during a free play situation and more interpersonal aggression during a frustrating situation.

Results differ when the measure of aggression is indirect. Two studies of elementary through middle-school children (Graybill *et al.* 1987; Winkel, Novak and Hopson 1987) found no relationship between playing violent video games and indirect measures of aggressive behaviour, such as money deducted from payment to an unseen 'student', actually a computer (Winkel, Novak and Hopson 1987). In a related vein, anger has been observed as one of the moods displayed by people playing fruit machines, particularly when the player has incurred consistent and sometimes heavy financial losses (Griffiths 1990). Fruit machine players can also get verbally aggressive towards the machine while playing (Griffiths 1989).

Video Games, Violence and Personality

Chapter Two showed that children's patterns of video game playing and game theme preferences were linked to personality characteristics. This leaves open a distinct likelihood that young players' subsequent behavioural reactions after playing these games could be mediated, in some degree, by their personalities. Mixed evidence has so far emerged that personality variables mediate adult responses to video games. Scott (1995) conducted a study on university students and found no differences in aggressive affect while playing video games on questionnaire scores on the Buss-Durkee Hostility Inventory (Buss and Durkee 1957) and the Eysenck Personality Questionnaire (Eysenck and Eysenck 1975) across varying levels of video game violence.

Gender differences in effects of video game play have been observed, but may depend on whether players compete as individuals or cooperate with others (Lightdale and Prentice 1994). There were no differences in male and female aggression when a video game was played cooperatively, but when players competed on their own, males were more aggressive than females. This finding reveals little about the relationship of video games and violence per se and suggests that any such link may depend on player gender and style of play. In another experiment that used video games to examine other theoretical concerns, Anderson, Deuser and DeNeve (1995) tested a general model of affective aggression via a study of video game playing. Using 107 undergraduate subjects, they manipulated the room temperature while subjects were playing the video games and found that raising the temperature consistently increased hostile affect and hostile cognition in players.

Irwin and Gross (1995) found that boys, aged seven and eight years, showed more aggressiveness when playing with other children, especially if another child did something to frustrate or annoy them, and displayed more violence towards inanimate objects in a play room if they had played a video game with a violent theme than one with a non-violent theme. The children were initially distinguished in terms of whether they could be categorized as reflective or impulsive in their cognitive style. There was no evidence, however, that this personality measure made any difference to the way the children behaved after playing with video games.

It could also be the case that the competitive nature of a video game may have an effect on aggression. To examine this, Anderson and Morrow (1995) extended and tested Deutsch's (1993) theory of competition effects using video games. The theory predicts that people view competitive situations as inherently more aggressive than they do co-operative ones. In a study of 60 undergraduates, competition primed subjects killed significantly more video game characters than co-operation primed subjects. The increased kill ratio occurred in the absence of changes of hostility, friendliness or liking for one's game partner.

Other research has examined children's and adolescents' video game play in relation to their self-concept. Harter (1986) developed a multi-dimensional theory of self-concept that envisages the self-concept as falling perceptually into a number of distinct areas or domains. Among the domains were identified: Scholastic Competence, Social Acceptance, Job Competence, Physical Appearance, Romantic Appeal, Behavioural Conduct, Athleticism Competence, Close Friendships and Global Self-Worth. A person might consider themselves to be competent in all these areas or in only one or two of them.

Using this approach Creasey and Vanden Avoind (1992) evaluated a sample of 25 children whose age and gender were unspecified. They reported that length of time playing video games was positively correlated with scores on the Harter subscale measuring perceived Athletic Competence. No differences were reported for any of the other subscales.

In a later study, Funk and Buckman (1996) tried to develop a system to measure game preference, to describe the current game-playing habits of young adolescents, and to examine the importance of a predisposition to violent games by exploring relationships among frequency and location of play, game preference and self-concept. The study was carried out among 357 adolescents aged 13 to 14 years.

Video games were placed into one of five categories: general entertainment, educational, sports, fantasy (cartoon) violence, or human violence (Funk 1993a). General entertainment games tell a story with no fighting or destruction, the main goal being to outmanoeuvre the video game. In educational games, acquiring and practising new knowledge is the main goal. Sports games include games with any type of sports action. In fantasy violence games, a cartoon or fantasy character must fight or destroy things in order to avoid being killed or destroyed while trying to reach a goal, rescue someone, or escape from something; the definition of human violence games is identical to that of fantasy violence games, except that the main character is a human figure.

Self-concept measures were not related to overall amount of time spent playing video or computer games either at home or in an arcade. Nor were they related to adolescents' stated preferences for fantasy or human violence games. There were differences between boys and girls, however, in video game playing and game preferences. Boys reported spending more time playing with electronic games at home and in arcades than did girls. Girls were more likely than boys to list fantasy violent games among their favourites, while boys exceeded girls in the extent to which they indicated preferences for games featuring human violence.

There were further gender differences in relation to the extent to which self-concept measures were predicted by video game playing. These relations occurred significantly only among girls, and not among boys. For girls, time spent playing video games in arcades was significantly linked with scores on Scholastic Achievement, Social Acceptance, and Athletic Competence. Time spent playing games at home was significantly linked to Behavioural Conduct scores. Both home and arcade game playing were linked to Global Self-Worth. Preferences for fantasy violent games was also linked to the Job Competence scale score. These results signified that the more time girls spent playing with video games the lower was their feeling of self-worth. The fantasy game preference, in contrast, was associated with a high sense of Job Competence.

The inverse relationships found between self-concept measures and video game playing were consistent with the notion of video game playing as a form of 'discounting'. Discounting is a behavioural phenomenon designed to preserve self-esteem (Harter 1986). However, such discounting may have a negative impact if competence in key areas drops below socially acceptable levels (Harter 1987).

Discounting may not be the key factor in each negative relationship between playing time and aspects of self-concept. For example, as with television viewing, game playing may directly lower academic achievement by displacing study time (van Evra 1990). Funk and Buckman (1996) accepted their participants' judgments of self-competence without additional measures and equated time spent playing electronic games with competence in game playing. This may not be the only explanation of the results though, and further independent measures of adolescent conduct may have helped to clarify the position.

At the present time, there is no firm indication that playing electronic games causes major adjustment problems for most players. Associations between game-playing habits and adjustment problems have been previously reported for sub-groups of players (Creasey and Vanden Avond 1992; Egli and Myers 1984; Ellis 1984). One interpretation of the Funk and Buckman results may be that a preference for violent electronic games is not significantly related to self-concept. The consistency of findings from related research on media violence, however, indicates that this question merits additional study (Donnerstein, Slaby and Eron 1994). Conclusions about the importance of a preference for violent games should be deferred pending further research. Although boys' time commitment was not associated with lower self-concept in the Funk and Buckman study, in at least one previous study a subgroup relationship was identified. Dominick (1984) reported a positive association between low self-esteem and solitary arcade play for young adolescent boys.

Other Research

Other studies have examined the possibility that playing video games, even those with violent themes, could have prosocial and beneficial effects on young viewers. Such effects may only be short-term, although their permanency remains to be established one way or the other. Research by Graybill and his associates reported that children, aged six to 11 years, exhibited fewer defensive fantasies and tended to show more assertive fantasies after playing violent video games, although this was a trend and not greatly significant. Aggression was assessed using a projective test—the Rosenzweig Picture-Frustration Study. The results were consistent with catharsis theory and indicated that video games with violent themes could provide a channel through which children can harmlessly discharge aggressive impulses (Graybill, Kirsch and Esselman 1985).

In another study, using a behavioural measure involving apparatus in which children could push buttons to hurt or help another child, and two self-report measures (the Response Hierarchy Measure and the Rosenzweig Picture-Frustration Study), there was no evidence that playing video games with violent or non-violent themes made much difference to the way children responded (Graybill *et al.* 1987).

In a more anecdotal account, Gardner (1991) claimed that the use of video games in his psychotherapy sessions provided common ground between himself and his client and provided excellent behavioural observation opportunities. Gardner described four particular case studies where video games were used to support psychotherapy and added that although other techniques were used as an adjunct in therapy (e.g. story telling, drawing, and other games) it was the video games that were the most useful factors in the improvement during therapy. He claimed that video games contributed to releasing and controlling aggression, although there was little evidence for this except for Gardner's own anecdotal observations.

The popularity of video games with violent and exciting themes has led to anxieties about their possible impact upon the behaviour of young people who regularly play these games. This reaction represents an extension of a more general and longer-term concern about the effects of media violence. This concern about the possible impact of the content of video games is further compounded by the observation that video games actively involve players in the action on screen in a way which watching television, for example, does not. So far, however, the research evidence on the effects of violent video games has been equivocal. Whether or not playing such games displays any manifest links with players' subsequent behavioural tendencies seems to vary with the type of research methodology deployed to investigate this question. Surveys of relationships between behavioural dispositions and video game play have revealed little consistent evidence of a link, while experimental paradigms have indicated that children may behave more aggressively in play situations after spending some time playing video games with violent themes. Even with experimental research, however, the results have varied with the types of operational measures of 'aggression' that have been used.

On the evidence to date, there is clearly a need for more research to be carried out with video games, which should perhaps focus on differentiating between various types of potential impact of video games, in relation to different types of game themes, production attributes and pre-existing player dispositions. Research with television violence has indicated that it is perhaps less informative to search for global effects than to investigate the potential of specific portrayals in particular programme contexts to act as trigger mechanisms sparking off undesirable reactions among audience members whose personalities and backgrounds predispose them to exhibit heightened sensitivities to such events on screen (Gunter 1985). In the following chapter, evidence on the potential health-related impact of video games indicates that some youngsters may be predisposed to react in a variety of particularly severe ways to video games, while under different contexts, video games can be used to benefit a young person's well being.

Chapter Six

Health Implications
of Playing Video Games

The popularity of computer and video games among children and teen-agers has produced some consideration of their possible health implications. There has been concern that excessive playing of these games not only affects players financially, but may also give rise to a host of adverse physical and psychological symptoms. Worries about the possible harms that may arise from playing these games are counter-balanced, to some extent, by findings that have shown that these games can be used constructively and purposefully to benefit children and teenagers with particular personal problems. In this chapter, evidence on both these types of effect is reviewed.

The Physical Consequences of Video Games

The medical profession has voiced a number of concerns about video game playing. According to Loftus and Loftus (1983), new kinds of aches and pains have been reported among players. Rheumatologists have described cases of 'Nintendinitis' and 'Space Invaders' Wrist' in which players have suffered skin, joint and muscle problems from repeated button hitting and joystick pushing on the game machines. In a survey by Loftus and Loftus, 65 per cent of (arcade) video game players exam-ined complained of blisters, calluses, sore tendons and numbness of fingers, hands and elbows directly as a result of their playing.

There have also been a number of case studies that have reported some of the adverse effects of playing (non-arcade) video games. These have included wrist pain (McCowan 1981), neck pain (Miller 1991), elbow pain (Bright and Bringhurst 1992), tensynvitis (also called 'Nintendi-nitis') (Reinstein 1983; Brassington 1990; Casanova and Casanova 1991; Siegal 1991), peripheral neuropathy (Friedland and St. John 1984), enuresis (Schink 1991), encoprisis (Corkery 1990), epileptic seizures (e.g., Rushton 1981; Dalquist, Mellinger and Klass 1983; Hart 1990) and even hallucinations (Spence 1993).

Some of these adverse effects were quite rare and 'treatment' simply involved cessation of playing of the games in question. In the cases involving enuresis and encoprisis, the children were so engaged in the games that they simply did not want to go to the toilet. In these particular cases they were taught how to use the game's 'pause' button.

Several specific case studies have been published in the American and British medical literature of individuals who have suffered muscle and joint pains and impairment of movement of certain joints as a result of playing video games intensively over both short and extended periods of time. McCowan (1981) reported his own experience of wrist pain after playing repeatedly with a friend's video games over a one month period. The games he played involved the use of a movable joystick or 'paddle' and required a large number of repetitive movements. The pain experienced disappeared after one and a half weeks abstinence from further play.

Other cases of aches and pains, and even temporary loss of use of joints, have been reported among adults who have played video games. Friedland and St. John (1984) reported the case of a 28-year-old man who lost the feeling in the medial two fingers of his left hand for two months after he had played video games four to six times a day for one month. While playing he had rested his left-hand on the machine and used his left fingers to turn a rotary knob. As with many video games, he had performed the same movements repeatedly a large number of times. The diagnosis of this medical problem was that during video game play, he had exerted undue and continual pressure on nerves responsible for controlling finger movements, such that they had temporarily ceased to function properly. Significant recovery from the problem occurred after three weeks of abstinence from video game play. Another case study, reported by the same writers, involved a 35-year-old woman who played with a Nintendo video game without interruption for five hours. The following day, she experienced severe pain in her right thumb, which had been used to press a button on the video game repeatedly. The pain disappeared after several days without further play.

Several cases have been reported of epileptic seizures among children and teenagers following video game play. These cases, though rare, resemble others in which seizures have been brought on by the fluttering of faulty television screens (e.g., Gastaut, Regis and Bostem 1962; Stefansson *et al.* 1977). One early observation of this phenomenon with video games occurred with a 17-year-old boy playing a game called *Astro Fighter*, which was judged to have the right size, brightness and frequently changing images, to cause seizures in susceptible individuals. In this case, the subject suffered epileptic attacks on two separate occasions after playing this particular game for 20 to 30 minutes (Rushton 1981).

Dahlquist and his colleagues (1983) reported a case of a 15-year-old boy with no previous history of seizures. He played video games regularly for one year before seizures began. On one occasion, it was observed that the boy appeared to be in a daze with his hand twitching while playing a game called *Combat*. A month or so later, the boy had a further seizure while playing a *Pacman* video game. Subsequently he developed a sensitivity to bright sunlight flickering through trees while being driven along a tree-lined road (Dalquist *et al.* 1983).

A further published case of video game-induced seizure involved a 13-year-old girl who had been playing a Nintendo game for three hours with only a short break. At a particularly rapid phase in the game, she reported feeling strange and then had a two to three minute seizure (Hart 1990). It appears that certain shifting patterns of images and light in video games can trigger seizures in photosensitive individuals. These cases, fortunately, are rare, but medical professionals have nevertheless given out warnings that video games may be capable of causing these reactions among children and teenagers who have a low tolerance for flashing lights and rapidly moving and changing images.

The Social Consequences of Video Games

Other speculative negative aspects of video game playing that have been reported include the belief that video game play is socially isolating and prevents children from developing social skills (e.g., Zimbardo 1982). One research has reported that video game players use the machines as 'electronic friends' (Selnow 1984). However, this does not necessarily mean that players play these games instead of forming human friendships and interacting with their peer groups. Indeed, some of the young people surveyed by Selnow indicated that going to video game arcades represented an important aspect of their social life. These arcades were meeting places and places to go to observe other people and to learn how other people behave and how to behave when with others.

This impression that video game arcades represent an important social environment was reinforced elsewhere. Colwell, Grady and Rhaiti (1995) reported that heavy video game players tended to see their friends more often outside school than did non-players, and had a need to see their friends on a regular basis. In fact, no difference has been found between high and low frequency video game players in terms of their inherent sociability (Rutkowska and Carlton 1994). Frequent players tend to enjoy just as many friendships and contacts with friends as do less frequent players (Phillips *et al.* 1995).

The social aspect of computer and video games can be experienced at home just as much as in arcades where on-line games are played. Multi-user Domains (MUDs) represent a broad class of on-line adventure games in which two or more participants can interact in fantasy virtual worlds that they can even help to create. By the mid-1990s one estimate calculated that 300 such games were in existence worldwide (Pavlik 1996) with scenarios ranging from mediaeval villages to science-fiction settings. For some observers and participants, MUDs are recognized as a major addiction among computer games players (Quittner 1994). Their allure has much to do with the psychological and social experience aforded by playing with MUDs. Regular users can establish relationships with other players, and through their involvement in MUDs can become members of virtual communities (Rheingold 1993).

In many ways, the virtual worlds created within MUDs have many of the social attributes of physical places. It is not unusual for regular users to treat the worlds produced by MUD programs as if they were real (Curtis 1992). Within a MUD, a user can meet new friends, forge close relationships, and enjoy an outlet in which to express their creativity and imagination. According to one writer:

> MUD environments are culturally rich and communication between MUD users is often highly emotionally charged. The means of expression open to users are limited by the technology on which MUDs are based, but instead of allowing that to restrict the content of their communication, users have devised methods of incorporating socioemotional context cues into pure language itself. They use text, seemingly such a restrictive medium, to make up for what they lack in physical presence. (Reid 1995: 167)

The MUD program represents a set of tools with which users can create a social and cultural environment in which a rich and varied range of communications with other people can be enjoyed. The anonymity that players enjoy, unless they choose voluntarily to give this up, leads to less inhibited communications than would be found in the real world. Players feel freer to speak their minds and vent their feelings without holding back as they probably would in face-to-face interactions with others (Kiesler and Sproull 1986; Kiesler, Siegel and McGuire 1984). Such disinhibition can be manifest in terms of greater aggressiveness and hostility or as greater friendliness and intimacy (Reid 1995). In such a computer-mediate environment, participants lack the nonverbal cues they would normally experience in real world environments when communicating with others, which often function to temper verbal and physical behaviours (Rice and Love 1987). This observation is challenged, however, by the fact that MUD users have developed nonverbal cues and signals even with text-based communications, and a lexicon of symbols that carry emotional connotations has been created for use alongside verbal language.

The usual convention of anonymity may be set aside when users wish to be identified during the course of establishing more intimate relationships with others. Such styles of communication may facilitate the development of true friendships between participants which have even been known to develop into romantic involvements.

> Virtual lovers use the commands with which the MUD system provides them to transform the virtual stage into a set designed to express and uphold their feelings for one another. The most common action taken by such partners is to set up virtual house together. They quite literally create a home together, using the MUD program to arrange textual information in a way that simulates a physical structure which they can then share and invite others to share. These relationships may even be consummated through virtual sex, enacted as co-written interactive erotica (Reid 1995: 175).

In contrast, MUDs can provide an environment in which open hostility is displayed. MUD systems can reduce self-consciousness and promote intimacy, but equally they can lead users to feel free to express anger and hatred. This can take the form of 'flaming', a phenomenon of computer-mediated communication that has been characterized as the gratuitous and uninhibited making of 'remarks containing swearing, insults, name calling and hostile comments' (Kiesler *et al.* 1984: 1129). Anonymity makes the possibility of everyday punishments appear to be limited. Open hostility is not generally accepted by MUD users as acceptable conduct, and systems usually have facilities that can be deployed to silence or banish disruptive users. It is clear that MUD systems break down some of the normal social barriers with consequent positive and negative side-effects. For individuals who may have difficulty establishing relationships through face-to-face encounters, however, these on-line computer games environments create a socially beneficial alternative in which they can feel more comfortable and self-confident.

Positive Benefits of Video Games

A growing body of literature has provided ample demonstration of the capability of video games to have real psychological benefits for young people. Some of this evidence derives from informal observations of game playing effects, while a number of studies have demonstrated the positive psychological value of these games in clinical treatment settings.

The positive effects of video games on cognitive skills may well extend to the development of social skills. One view is that youngsters who play video games can enhance their social relationships through doing so, especially when they go to arcades to play them with others of their own age group (Favaro 1982). These positive social benefits are not restricted to arcade games. In a study of the impact of home video on family life, Mitchell (1985) reported that families generally felt video games promoted family interaction in a beneficial way through creating situations for cooperation among family members as well as gentle competitiveness between them. Concerns that the growing popularity of home videos might produce a generation of lonely and withdrawn children who have no other interests have not been borne out by research evidence so far. Creasey and Myers (1986) assessed the impact of home video games on children's leisure activities, school work and peer contacts. They found that none of these three activities was affected by the presence of video games in the home, nor by the regular playing of them.

One positive benefit of playing video games, according to some writers, is that the self-motivated mastery of a game can lead to an improved sense of self-worth on the part of the player. The playing of popular video games has been delineated into a number of stages that represent a continuing evolution of the relationship between the game and player. In the beginning, the rules are learned, Next, these rules are evaluated and judged. Lastly, the rules (if deemed worthy) are adopted by the player (Myers 1984). As the player proceeds through these stages of identifying, assessing and adopting rules of play, there are complementary social benefits derived from the experience.

The use of computer games has been found to aid the development of intellectual growth and social interaction, whether used educationally or as entertainment (see Loftus and Loftus 1983). Egli and Meyers (1984) found that arcades acted as social centres and places for the development of friendship, in a similar manner to Shotton's computer game dependents who made contact and friendships with others in order to share and copy games software (see Chapter Three). Since playing computer games involves a challenge between the player and software, and not between the player and another person, computer games-playing was found to decrease competitiveness and to increase cooperativeness (Bowman 1982). It also provided an ideal environment for the development of competence, self-determination and status.

Video games can be used as training aids for certain cognitive and perceptual-motor disorders (Lynch 1981). These disorders can be found in patients who have been in accidents, have had strokes, or who have simply been born with such problems. Loftus and Loftus (1983) reported the case of a teenage girl who suffered brain damage after being involved in a car accident. This damage manifest itself in terms of a sudden inability to spell (spelling dyspraxia). Video game therapy was used on a twice-weekly basis to treat the disorder. This mostly involved playing a game called *Hangman* in which two people guess letters in a word. If a correct letter appears, there is no penalty. If an incorrect letter appears, another portion of the 'hangman' is added on. After two months of this treatment, the dyspraxia problem was significantly reduced.

By the early 1980s, a number of video game therapy centres had appeared across the United States. Video games were used to treat a variety of cognitive disorders with some success. One particular advantage of this technique was that much of the treatment could be carried out at the patient's own home, to which the video game being used in therapy could be delivered.

The Therapeutic Value of Video Games

For a long time, therapists working with children have used games as an aspect of child therapy in relation to the treatment of a wide range of psychological problems (Gardner 1991). Play has been a feature of therapy since the work of Anna Freud (1928) and Melanie Klein (1932) and has been used to promote fantasy expression and the ventilation of feeling.

The rapid evolution of new technologies which have been felt with particular effect on the home entertainment front, has brought a proliferation of new computer-based games that some therapists have adopted as tools in the therapeutic process. Such games have been found to be especially effective with young patients, serving as an excellent way to establish a rapport with the therapist and to control and shape behaviour (Spence 1988; Gardner 1991).

According to Gardner (1991), the application of video games in his psychotherapy sessions provided common ground between himself and his client and provided excellent behavioural observation opportunities. These opportunities allowed Gardner to observe:

(1)   the child's repertoire of problem-solving strategies;

(2)   the child's ability to perceive and recall subtle cues as well as foresee consequences of behaviour and act on past consequences;

(3)   eye-hand coordination;

(4)   the release of aggression and control;

(5)   the ability to handle in a mature fashion the joys of victory and frustrations of defeat in a more sports-oriented arena;

(6)   the satisfaction of effective deployment of cognitive skills in the recall of bits of basic information;

(7)   the enjoyment of mutually coordinating one's activities with another person in the spirit of cooperation.

Gardner went on to describe four particular case studies where video games were used to support psychotherapy and added that although other techniques were used as an adjunct in therapy (e.g. story-telling, drawing, other games and so on) it was the video games that were the most useful factors in the improvements observed during therapy.

Gardner contended that clinical techniques tend to change as a function of the trends of the times, even though the end goals remain the same. Slower-paced and more traditional procedures may lengthen the time it takes to form a therapeutic relationship, because the child may perceive the therapist not to be 'with it'.

During the mid-1980s, researchers found that video games could facilitate cooperative behaviour among children and be used to reinforce desirable conduct within educational settings (Stein and Kochman 1984; Salend and Santora 1985).

There have been a number of innovative uses of video games in therapeutic contexts. 'Video game therapy' was used by Lynch (1981 1983) for various types of mental disorder (e.g. stroke patients). Not only can video game performance be compared between patients and 'normals', but video game playing can be used as a training aid to some cognitive and perceptual-motor disorders. Further to this, Szer (1983) reported the case of using video game playing as physiotherapy for someone with an arm injury and Phillips (1991) reported the case of using a hand-held video game (Nintendo *Game Boy*) to stop an eight-year-old boy picking at his face. In this latter case, the child had enurodermatitis and scarring due to continual picking at his upper lip. Previous treatment had included a brief behaviour modification programme with food rewards for periods free of picking and the application of a bitter tasting product to the child's fingers. These failed to work, so Phillips recommended the use of a hand-held video game which was a psychologically rewarding experience and kept the boy's hands occupied. After two weeks the affected area had healed and at a two-month follow-up, Phillips reported no problems related to the child's continued use of the game.

Video games have been applied to the treatment of young people with a variety of handicaps. Horn, Jones and Hamlett (1991) examined the effectiveness of a video game format in training three children, aged between five and eight years, with multiple handicaps (e.g. severely limited vocal speech acquisition) to make scanning and selection responses similar to those needed to operate communication aids manufactured to assist them with their speech difficulties. The video scanning and selection game systematically shaped their behaviour which involved selecting from among a number of boxes containing words. Playing this game produced improvements in the ability of the children to perform this task, which was subsequently found to transfer well to the application of a similar skill needed to operate a communication device.

Video games may provide a distraction or an escape from worry and painful situations or feelings, having both physical and psychological benefits for young people. There are also many reports (e.g. Kolko and Rickard-Figueroa 1985; Redd *et al.* 1987; Vasterling *et al.* 1993) that video games have been used as a diversion from the side effects of cancer chemotherapy during childhood and that such distraction tasks can reduce the amount of pain killers needed by the children.

At a psychological level, evidence has emerged that video games can alleviate feelings of anxiety. In one study, physiological and psychological measures of anxiety were taken of female college students, around half of whom were preclassified as having highly anxious personalities, and half as being relatively calm. While the high anxiety women were more likely to report being anxious throughout the experiment, physiological measures of skin conductance revealed that their arousal level actually decreased while they were playing a video game. For non-anxious women, no such effect was observed (Naveteur and Ray 1990).

Spence (1988) was another advocate of the therapeutic value of video games and incorporated them into his repertoire of behaviour management techniques. Spence believed that video games could be used instrumentally to bring about changes in a number of areas and provided case study examples for each of these changes.

(1) *Development of relationships.* Video games can be used to provide the basis to develop a therapeutic relationship. Spence found that video games could provide an acceptable middle ground for both parties to meet which provided an enjoyable experience for therapist and patient. The therapeutic relationship thus became a close and trusting one.

(2) *Motivation.* Video games could be used as bargaining counters to motivate children to do things. This simply involved negotiating with an individual for a set period of work time or tasks in return for a set period of time playing video games.

(3) *Cooperative behaviour.* Video games could be used to develop social skills and cooperation in individuals by making them share a video with peers. Through the medium of video games, individuals developed friendships which fostered cooperation.

(4)   *Aggressive behaviour.* Video games could be deployed to take the heat out of situations. Thus, individuals played video games when they were angry so that the damage was inflicted on the games' characters, rather than on other individuals.

(5)   *Self-esteem.* Video games were used as a measure of achievement to raise self-esteem. Since video games are skill-based and provide scores, they can be compared and provide a basis for future goals. Breaking personal high scores raised self-esteem in the individual.

Other reports of the application of commercially available computer software to the therapeutic context have indicated that positive results can be obtained. Computer games have been recommended for their capabilities to provide distinctive help in overcoming certain therapeutic problems in a form of treatment to which adolescents will readily respond. Such computer-based games have recently been found to offer satisfactory treatment solutions for even quite complex therapeutic problems among adolescent patients. One such illustration was the development of an adventure-based computer game for the treatment of adolescents with difficulty controlling sudden impulses to behave in unusual or anti-social ways (Clarke and Schoech 1994).

Video adventure games and games involving fantasy role-playing can be used effectively to train adolescents to deal with real-life situations that have been simulated in the games, by creating scenarios that may not exist in the adolescent's own life experience. Mystery computer games can be used with good results when working with groups of adolescents suffering psychiatric problems. The group can learn by observing and modelling the behaviour of group leaders as well as by participating in the development of successful problem-solving strategies (Favelle 1994).

Even with young children, successful therapeutic applications have been reported. In one study, an ordinary office personal computer loaded with a role playing game, an electronic play programme, a programme that combined a simple word processor with a collection of pictures to produce cartoon-type stories, and a game of explanation suitable for pre-schoolers was used to conduct play therapy with children (Kokush 1994). Throughout, the software applied was low-cost and commercially available. Case examples illustrated the use of such PC-based programmes in a small, private practice. The therapeutic progression of the young clients and their relationship with the therapist were described. Successful treatments were reported, but not without problems along the way. On balance, however, computer-based games were found to be a useful addition to the therapeutic tool-kit of the child therapist.

Social and Health Awareness Promotion

In recent years, computer games and simulations have been developed to assist promotional and educational campaigns aimed to put across social and health-related messages to children and adolescents. Bosworth (1994) reported the use of these technologies in a comprehensive health promotion campaign aimed at adolescents. They were used to attract the attention to young people to BARN (Body Awareness Resource Network) as well as to hold their interest across the duration of the campaign. This programme comprised six topic areas: AIDS, alcohol, other drugs, body management, human sexuality, smoking and stress management. Quiz games challenged players to test their knowledge on a topic. Simulations challenged users to apply health information in nonjudgmental, hypothetical situations. The games played an important part in turning young people's attention on to this health campaign and worked equally well among frequent and infrequent video game players

Cahill (1994) reported on research with *Health Works*, a prototype AIDS education programme developed by the New York State Department of Health for schoolchildren aged between 11 and 14 years. *Health Works* featured state-of-the-art interactive computer video programmes and animated graphics on five stand-alone computer stations, housed in a customised mobile unit. Between January 1989 and June 1992 *Health Works* was visited by more than 17,000 students at 172 schools in New York State, including new York City. Cahill analyzed results concerning its impact for over 3,800 New York City students.

The findings revealed that video games can take students beyond straightforward factual learning to a deeper involvement with the subject matter, having a much more powerful impact on strength of learning and likelihood of adoption of recommended health-related behaviours. The Health Works visits to schools served as booster sessions for classroom AIDS education.

Another computer-based programme was developed around the same time to campaign against the use of drugs. Oakley (1994) described the development and utilization of SMACK, a computer-driven game for teenagers, which addressed drug abuse. The game was developed to illustrate to teenagers the negative consequences associated with drug use. The game was comprised of simulations requiring teenagers to make decisions regarding drug use and to respond to the consequences of such decisions. It was found that the programme reinforced the anti-drug attitude of teens who were not inclined towards drug use.

Other games have been developed to assist with the moral development of young people and the rehabilitation of those who have already become offenders. The development and application of a computerized therapeutic simulation game for raising the moral level of adolescents or to resocialize those who had already got into trouble was described by Sherer (1994). The effects of the game on moral development were determined by a moral development measure. The level of moral development of 13 teenagers who participated in this exercise and 14 others who served as a comparison group, all aged 15 years, was measured before and after exposure to the therapeutic game. Participants met for 16 weekly, two-hour sessions in which the first hour was spent playing with the computer game followed by a further hour of discussion. Two out of five indices of moral development were found to show improvements as a result of playing with the computer game. Counsellors reported that the teenagers had been stimulated by the computer game experience, while the teens themselves enjoyed the games and thought they were relevant to the issues being addressed.

A computer simulation game called BUSTED was designed as part of a programme to reduce antisocial behaviour in young offenders. The aim of this game was to raise delinquents' awareness of their own conduct and the consequences of antisocial behaviour for victims, and to work on these youngsters' interpersonal skills when dealing with other people. The rehabilitation programme using this game ran for three to four weeks, during which it was played once or twice a week for around one and a half hours a time by three to six players. The game set up scenarios in which players had to take decisions, make choices and receive the consequences of those choices. Firm conclusions about the effectiveness of BUSTED have not yet been reached and its evaluation is still continuing. A preliminary evaluation conducted in two high school classrooms yielded positive results, with both boys and girls showing a degree of enthusiasm for the game and claiming to have learned something from it. Teachers also reportedly found the programme useful. Whether it can produce longer-term attitudinal and behavioural changes remains to be seen. Nevertheless, this project represents one more illustration of the way computer games are being applied to problems relating to children's and adolescents' social and moral development (Sherer 1994).

Video games can have both positive and negative health implications. Clinical observations have revealed that certain types of video games coupled with intensive playing of them, can give rise to adverse physiological reactions, causing epileptic seizures among individuals with such a predisposition as well as producing physical strains, aches and pains deriving from bad posture or repetitive movements during play. Counterbalancing these problems, however, is evidence that playing video games can have positive benefits for youngsters in the sense of boosting feelings of self worth and in the context of treating behavioural disorders. As with many other forms of home entertainment, video games need to be used sensibly in a carefully managed fashion. Where they represent part of a social scene for young people, their use seems to be generally controlled and related to positive feelings about self. Where they are used as a social distraction and a form of escape or withdrawal from social contact, they represent part of an undesirable behavioural syndrome which needs to be discouraged. The key to their health-related effects lies to a significant extent with the personality of the individual and his (and less often her) reasons for playing.

Chapter Seven

Future Implications
for the Computer Generation

The past 20 years have witnessed an explosive growth in the playing of computer or video games, both in and out of the home. Vast sums of money are spent every year by games arcades and private consumers on purchasing the hardware and software for these games, spawning a massive, and highly profitable international entertainment industry. The power of the video game appeal lies principally in its interactive nature. Unlike traditional forms of audio-visual entertainment, and most especially television, video games involve players to the extent that they interact with and exert a degree of control over the events that occur on screen. The most popular games are liked best because they offer extra special challenges to players' skills and engage their minds in the action to such an extent that the games provide a powerful distraction from everyday cares. Computer and video games represent the first digital media technology to socialize a generation on a mass scale, with the great majority of teenagers in developed countries having some experience of playing them (Johnstone 1993). Computer and video games carry the sort of significance and meaning to the current generation of young people that cinema and television did to past generations (Wark 1994).

The home video game market has been one of the fastest growing areas of home entertainment in the last two decades. From their appearance in the late 1970s, cartridge-based home video games machines have developed extremely rapidly. Software for these games has been marketed aggressively, particularly by such manufacturers as Sega and Nintendo. These two companies are continuing to develop ever more sophisticated games machines with greater and greater computer power. Sega have even begun to take these developments a stage further by entering the interactive, down-the-line video market. The Sega Channel is an innovative use of multimedia and cable distribution, offering consumers an opportunity to try out demonstration versions of new software releases by downloading them over cable networks. The significance of these computer games companies lies in their hybrid nature. They are neither pure toy companies nor pure computer companies, but a mixture of toy, computer and media operation (Humphries 1993; Johnstone and Howell 1991). Digital media technology inter-relates media forms that were once separate, causing an overlap between the markets once held as separate competitive and operational domains by broadcasters, computer manufacturers and publishers (Brand 1987; Negroponte 1993).

Video Games: More than Just Entertainment

The significance of the video game phenomenon, however, does not simply reside in the extent to which it has captured a huge following, particularly among young people, but also in the psychological nature of game playing. Computer and video games require certain mental skills and digital dexterity on the part of players. Being computer-based, the games serve as an initial introduction to the world of computers, which may be readily accepted by the younger generation as a natural part of the cultural environment; something to be accepted rather than feared. More than this, though, playing video games involves particular patterns of information processing and psychological reaction to events occurring on screen. The style and speed of play demands a degree of cognitive versatility on the part of the player who reaches an advanced level with regular practice. These 'cognitive' skills, which tend to be related more closely to the assimilation and interpretation of information presented in pictures rather than words, are and will continue to be, an increasingly important form of learning and understanding in a world where computers are at the centre of so much of what goes on in business, education and entertainment.

Video Games: A Major Social Problem?

Like many new forms of entertainment that attract widespread public appeal, the video games phenomenon has given rise to concerns about possible adverse side effects that they might have on those who get heavily involved with them (McKee 1992; Billen 1993). These concerns have become particularly acute because of the popularity of video games with children and teenagers. Critical and cautionary remarks about video games have not just appeared in newspaper articles; even academic publications have emerged that questioned whether they could be regarded as a psychologically healthy pastime for young people (Loftus and Loftus 1983; Provenzo 1991). The public anxieties surrounding these games stem principally from two main concerns, the first of which is linked to the amount of time children play with these games, and the second of which is connected with the nature of many of the games themselves. Video games are seen as potentially harmful when children spend time playing them to the neglect of other educational, social and leisure activities. The main worries here are that video games take time away from doing homework, general reading, or playing sports. There is the additional suggestion that children who really become hooked on these games tend to play alone and eschew social contact. The concerns about the games themselves stem from the observation that many games have violent and anti-social themes, which may create more impulsive and aggressive tendencies among those who play these games a great deal.

One content analysis of video games found recurring themes of gender-stereotyping, aggression and violence. More than nine in ten games analysed (92 per cent) had no female characters at all, while among the remainder, six per cent featured women as damsels in distress, and just two per cent featured 'action women' characters (Provenzo 1991). One significant observation is not simply that video games commonly contain violence, but that the violence generally occurs devoid of any narrative context or storyline. As Provenzo observes: 'The lone individual setting out on a quest is not a new theme in western culture, but such tales usually are leavened with pathos or tragedy ... video games lack (any) moral counterweight' (1991: 56).

Violent video games do not always receive a warm welcome from the markets they attempt to penetrate and controls are implemented by national regulators, either to restrict or to block access to particular age groups where question-marks hang over the tastefulness of their content, or potential psychological harm such games may cause among young players. One of Sega's CD-ROM games, *Night Trap*, triggered controversy over its depiction of teenage girls at a pyjama party who are abducted by zombies. Zombie violence included striking a claw-like appendage against their victim's neck. The game was banned in Britain for anyone under 15, and major retail chains such as Toys R Us in Britain and Canada refused to sell the game. Finally, under pressure from the US Congress and children's advocates, Sega pulled the game out of the market (Brandt, Gross and Coy 1994).

As we have seen from the evidence reviewed in this book, many of these worries are unfounded. There is no doubt that video games are played far and wide and that many young people have at least some experience of playing them either at home or in arcades. The amount of time spent actually playing, though, has often been over-stated (Egli and Meyers 1984). In arcades, for example, even the keenest players do not spend all their time sitting in front of a console. Arcades represent social gathering places for young people, many of whom spend as much time talking to their friends and watching others play as playing themselves (Michaels 1993). Even those who play at home, do not spend all their time playing. Children who play video games regularly have rarely showed signs of experiencing greater difficulties making friends (Shimai, Masuda and Kishimoto 1990; Schie and Wiegman 1996).

Some children may admit to playing more than they think they should, but few signs have emerged so far that video game addiction is a growing social problem. Video game players do not differ significantly from non-players in terms of other activities, including sports (Phillips *et al.* 1995). Clearly there may be some young people, whose personalities may predispose them to have difficulties making friends or engaging confidently with other people, for whom video games represent a form of escape. So far, there has been little evidence to suggest that these youngsters are anything more than a rarity (Gibb *et al.* 1983) and there are no indications that the presence of video games is causing this group to expand.

What is needed is a more positive and constructive outlook where computer and video games are concerned. This is not an invitation to complacency. Nor is it being suggested that we should have no concerns about these games at all. As with any other evolving entertainment medium, their progress needs to be monitored to be sure that games are not produced in which the contents push beyond the boundaries of social acceptability and good taste. As video games become even more readily available through cable television systems which can deliver them straight into the player's home (Miller 1996), there is a need for continued vigilance in the way they are used both from an economic cost and child health point of view. Nevertheless, research evidence is accumulating from a growing body of enquiry into the early impact of these games, which shows that playing them engages and cultivates a range of important cognitive abilities and skills that may transfer from game playing to other computer-related and non-computer-related learning or problem-solving tasks. Furthermore, some experts have argued that because video games generally require players to learn the rules and strategies of the game through trial-and-error, they may develop the type of mental attitude and style of thought which typifies and is needed for effective scientific enquiry (Greenfield 1994). Furthermore, in a world increasingly dominated by computers and requiring of people generally a higher degree of computer literacy, video games can, through the cognitive skills they demand, serve to play an important part in children's and adults' intellectual and social development in the new information technology era (Thomas and Macredie 1995).

Realizing the Educational Potential of Video Games

The appeal of video games to children is something that can be utilized to advantage in educational contexts. By investigating the production features of these games in order to identify which aspects motivate the player's concentration and commitment, it should be possible to adapt some of the techniques to produce learning packages for situations in which a high level of motivation is needed. A number of early studies attempted to carry out this kind of analysis of video games and were able to identify several key attributes and ingredients. Some of these features were more clearly linked to specific production features than others, however, and consequently vary in their degree of usefulness in drawing up a schema to aid the design of educational materials.

In one of the earliest studies, Malone (1981) listed the motivational aspects of video games under three categories: challenge, fantasy and curiosity. These elements were derived from interviews with young players about their personal video game experiences, preferences and opinions. Other investigators went beyond the identification of motivational attributes of video games and attempted to build educational computer games in which these features were incorporated. In one such exercise, three experimental computer games were designed to improve reading skills, which incorporated the motivational features of video arcade games (Fredericksen *et al.* 1982). The features cited as important and as being potentially transferable to educational computer instruction were: clear-cut goals, fast pace, immediate feedback and variable levels of challenge. Unfortunately, the authors of this framework did not explain how they had arrived at these production elements.

A clearer explication of educational computer games development was offered by another research group (Chaffin, Maxwell and Thompson 1982). On this occasion, six educational game formats based on entertainment-oriented video game styles, were developed, dealing with basic arithmetic skills called *Academic Skillbuilders*. These games were designed after a careful, systematic examination of video game contents, and observations of and interviews with video game players. Through this analysis, four motivational features were identified: (1) feedback; (2) improvement; (3) high response rate; and (4) unlimited ceilings on performance.

Feedback was an essential element. Players of video games like to know immediately whether a particular response was correct or incorrect, appropriate or inappropriate on that occasion, and likely to take them on successfully to the next stage or not. Incorrect responses are generally not explained; players have to work this out for themselves through a process of trial-and-error and deductive reasoning. Improvement represents a fact relating to the rate and staging of better performance at a game. In normal learning contexts, a steady rate of improvement is usually expected when practising a task. With video games, players typically do poorly on the first few games, but such is the challenge to do better that is cultivated by the games themselves, that early failure tends not to cause players to give up. Instead, they generally try even harder to master the game. Initial experiences, therefore, are mainly concerned with gaining familiarity with the game and how it is played. It is important to remember that these games are not usually accompanied by written instructions. Players have to learn how to play them through practice. Gradually, players learn to identify and implement correct strategies.

Video games tend to require a *high response rate* of possibly several hundred responses for a good performance. With such high response rates (perhaps 30 to 100 per minute), there is no room for distracting thoughts and a high level of concentration is required. With computer-based educational packages, a similar process of rapid responding is needed to ensure continued attention and interest. Finally, there must be an *unlimited ceiling on performance*, meaning that as with video games, there must be a successive levels of difficulty. As one level of difficulty is mastered, another higher level must be introduced so that there is always another challenge. This unlimited ceiling allows players to continue to improve their skills as their coordination and response times get better and as they employ more effective strategies. In an educational programme, students are required to master a given stage of difficulty before moving on to a higher level. Students who can respond at high speed, however, will create more time and opportunities for further practice. Rapid feedback will enable students to link their performance more readily with their responses, and to work on ways, where necessary, of correcting their performance. As students become proficient, the unlimited ceiling idea will continue to stretch them beyond traditional levels of mastery.

Video Games as a Form of Computer Training

There is a developing view that computer games contain design features and teach skills that can be usefully applied in other aspects of human-computer interaction. One key aspect of computer or video games is that they tend to provide virtual representational worlds in which activities similar to those which might be carried out in the real world may be simulated. Unlike real world situations, however, in which unskilled practitioners may be trained, mistakes have no real impact. Thus simulated, computer-generated situations that model real world environments provide an opportunity for individuals to acquire skills and learn strategies in the safe knowledge that errors will not have any real world implications. Such training situations may be especially important if such virtual reality learning produces skills that readily transfer across into equivalent real world environments.

Taking this reasoning a stage further, computer games may provide environments in which skills can be developed, acquired and practised in respect of developing yet more effective virtual reality simulations for real world skills training. The closer to the real world a virtual world can get in terms of its various key characteristics, the more effective it will be as a training tool. The real world is often a complex place and the development of accurate computer simulations, which can resemble reality in all its finer details, requires ever more powerful and complex computing systems. Such systems, while becoming more complex however, must not become so difficult to use that learners become demotivated. Creating user-friendly and yet complex virtual worlds may, according to some experts, benefit from the kind of computer system design features which appear in many video games (Malone 1980; Carroll 1982; Carroll and Mack 1984; Carroll and Thomas 1988; Neal 1990; Rivers 1990).

One important feature of video games, which is regarded as crucial in the design of complex computer systems, is their ability to motivate users, in an intrinsic sense, to persevere in learning how to play games even when no written instructions have been provided, and to keep playing so as to improve the skill level at which a particular game is played. Attempts to identify and classify these intrinsic motivational components have indicated that the key features in this context include the challenge posed by a game, with players having to progress through varying levels of difficulty in mastering it; a fantasy element in which players can act out make-believe roles and activities; and a curiosity-stimulating attribute whereby players have to engage in a venture of discovery in order to uncover hidden features of game play (Malone 1980, 1981a, 1981b). Video games can also motivate players by continually presenting new situations and problems, challenging the intellect of players by setting up problems that may not always be straightforward to solve, and introducing unexpected elements and varying degrees of uncertainty about outcomes (Malone and Lepper 1987; Rivers 1990). Video games also set goals and objectives for players, giving them something to aim for. This feature often occurs in a context of competition, where the player may be pitched against another player or against the machine itself. All these features are important to generating and maintaining intrinsically motivating environments (Neal 1990).

Exploratory research in which individuals were videotaped while they played at length with four computer games (*Mystery Box, ThinkAhead, Crystal Quest* and *Tetris*) indicated that games have considerable and immediate relevance for the design of more general human-computer interfaces (Neal 1990). By inviting players to think aloud while playing these games, it was possible to identify a variety of features, typical of computer or video games, which played an important role in encouraging players to continue playing even when faced with difficult problems or obstacles to progress.

The important question to ask in this context is whether video game techniques can be directly and effectively transferred to other computer design environments, or whether they merely demonstrate design principles that need to be adapted idiosyncratically to distinct computer environments. One school of thought is that a certain level of adaptation is needed and that interactive computer interfaces can rarely mimic video game design features in any direct sense and hope to be effective (Thomas and Macredie 1995). The chief reasons for this limitation in generalizability are that there is a cultural division between work and recreational uses of computers; the motivational effect of video games is usually transient rather than long-lasting; and there are different types of usage for computers and design features need to take into account subtle differences between applications and the needs of users in those situations. The significance of computer or video games lies in their application as software package training tools for users of different computer applications. Game features can be exploited in situations where users have only short exposure to training packages, by assisting in enhancing the rapid acquisition of basic principles (Thomas and Macredie 1995).

The recreational aspect of video games has not universally been regarded as a hindrance to their effectiveness in guiding the design of computer-assisted learning systems. The value of play in providing a healthy learning climate, particularly in the context of multimedia learning environments has been recently brought into clearer focus (Rieber 1996). The microworlds created by computer software designers can be enhanced in their ability to maintain the interest of users, whether they are children or adults, if they offer clear and simple goals with uncertain outcomes, and new challenges to keep users on their toes. Gradually increasing layers of complexity serve to stretch users to an optimal degree, such that once they have reached one level of competence they are pushed towards another, higher level. Each successive level of complexity, however, is not so far removed from the preceding one that it runs the risk of causing disillusionment, because for some users it proves to be excessively difficulty to achieve. Once achieved, feedback on the user's success is immediate, allowing users quickly to evaluate their progress. These are basic features of video games and have relevance to other computer interface applications.

Classifying Video Games

In determining the impact of video games on children and teenagers it is important to examine the nature of the content and predominant themes of these games. There has understandably been concern about the nature and prevalence of violent themes. There are good reasons for a closer analysis of the possible effects of violent video games. Video game violence is different from television violence. The differences have a positive and potentially negative side to them. On the one hand, video game violence has tended to be more abstract in nature, analogous to the kind of televised violence found in cartoons or fantasy science fiction or super-hero type programmes (Dominick 1984). However, there are recent signs that video game violence is changing to become more realistic (Provenzo 1991). In particular, a distinction can be made between the newer martial arts games and the earlier space wars type. As one writer remarked: 'There is a significant difference between shooting a series of stylized and abstracted spaceships, as is the case in the classic video game *Invaders*, and throwing body blocks and head kicks in martial arts games, such as *Double Dragon*, *Bad Dudes* or *Shinobi*' (Provenzo 1991: 67). Although the same writer goes on to add: 'Whether these games encourage more aggressive behaviour in their users needs to be determined by future research' (p. 67).

Another factor characteristic of video games, on the other hand, which distinguishes them from television, is that they are interactive and the players can control events on screen. This means that players may get more emotionally involved in the action on screen than would be the case with a television programme. Particular concern has been reserved for the most recent game developments involving virtual reality. Such games, in which the player can determine precise shape of on-screen behaviour by acting out movements in front of the screen, invite an even greater level of involvement in the game than standard keyboard, joystick or mouse operated computer games (Provenzo 1991).

The notion that all video games are alike or consist mostly of ones with violent themes is a misleading impression that persists in the public domain among people unfamiliar with the product range that is available. According to the magazine *Computer Gaming World*, by 1992 about 4000 computer games had been published, together with thousands more games more generally available in the public domain on a non-commercial basis (Wilson 1992). These products ranged from arcade style games emphasizing hand-eye coordination to role-playing games adding graphics and sound to an adventure-oriented formula, to simulation games in which players oversee the growth and development of systems ranging from cities to galaxies to alternate life forms.

Video games come in many varieties and cover a number of distinct themes. Nevertheless, it has been recognised by those who have studied the subject that there is a need for a general taxonomy of video games. This would help to determine which games, potentially, could have beneficial effects and which ones might have neutral or adverse effects on players. Studies of the educational potential of computer game technology have tried to specify the ingredients that lie at the core of successful educational interactive audio-visual productions. These exercises, however, have produced fairly limited typologies, which are narrowly focused upon a particular application of the technology. *Computer Gaming World*, for example, divided the contemporary field, as seen in 1992, into seven genres: action/arcade, adventure, role-playing adventure, simulation, sports, strategy and war. Within these categories, however, there was much overlap. An empire-building game such as *Civilization*, for instance, rests somewhere between a war game and a simulation game (Myers 1989).

Video games can be classified in a variety of ways along a number of dimensions. The creation of a comprehensive and helpful typology should probably begin by trying to identify what those key defining and distinguishing attributes and dimensions are. Distinctions between games can be made on the basis of their fundamental aims, how they are played, and their thematic qualities. One broad distinction has been in terms of whether the games are designed principally for entertainment purposes or whether they have an educational orientation. Games with varying graphic and action elements have been designed to teach a variety of educational subjects (Burton and Brown 1979; Char 1983; Dugdale and Kibbey 1982; Piestrup 1982; Robinett 1982; Wood 1980). Other video games have been studied from the perspective of the effects they have on the development of particular cognitive skills (Burbules and Reese 1984; Stein and Linn 1985; Greenfield 1983, 1993, 1994). Even games with an entertainment orientation have been investigated in terms of their educational potential (Chaffin, Maxwell and Thompson 1982; Mick *et al.* 1983; Greenfield, Camaioni *et al.* 1994).

A second key distinction centres on the way they engage the player's involvement. One distinction that has been made is between arcade games and role-playing games (Myers 1984). The term 'arcade' game is used here to apply not just to games situated in arcades, but also to a certain category of home video game (with certain arcade-game characteristics) which can be loaded onto a home computer. Thus, arcade games, as defined here, refer to games that require more manual dexterity than strategic thought. These games are reflex games and require the player to react instantly rather than offering the time to reflect on the next move. These games demand speed, accuracy and flexibility of play so as to deal effectively with often rapidly changing and uncertain developments on screen.

In contrast to this, role-playing games require relatively little manual dexterity. Moves are entered through a keyboard (as opposed to a paddle or joystick) and almost always require much more information than is displayed by the game on the screen at any one particular moment. While arcade-style games are centred on iconic (graphical or pictorial) displays, role-playing games have more verbal content. According to Myers: 'Arcade games require that the players react in a predictable manner *within* time; role-playing requires that the players react in a predictable manner *over* time, thereby discovering the inherent dynamic, dramatic patterns of the game software and simultaneously constructing a game *history*' (1984: 163).

The same writer went on to draw distinctions between three types of role-playing game: (1) the *puzzle/maze* role-playing game; (2) the *adventure/drama* role-playing game; and (3) the *multiplayer/competitive* role-playing game. With puzzle games, the player must proceed step-by-step towards the correct solution or end-goal. Along the way, mistakes are punished by players being 'killed' or unable to proceed any further, and must therefore begin the game all over again. With this type of game, however, once the puzzle has been solved or the maze has been run, there may be little incentive to continue playing. The entertainment value derives from initial attempts to crack the code.

The adventure game may also involve the running of a course with obstacles placed in the player's path, but much more emphasis is placed on the characters in the game. Whereas in most arcade games, the player is represented by a dot on the screen, in adventure games the player assumes the role of a game character shown on screen. Some of the games in this category allow the role-playing aspect to develop by permitting the player to build a character by assigning different characteristics to him. The character may also get a name and a profession, which can be chosen by the player. Characters can be good or bad, weak or strong, kind or mean. As the complexity of the character profiles and storylines increase, so the number of different options or course of action open to the player increase, adding layer upon layer of difficulty and challenge to the game.

The competitive game that can be played by more than one player at a time, adds a significant new dimension—a second human input. These games are very often computerized imitations of established board games (such as Monopoly), or simulations of real-life competitions (usually with sports or war themes). Such games tend to proceed at a pace. The player's opponent is another player rather than the computer, with the computer in this context acting as referee and/or score keeper.

Video games can also be distinguished in terms of thematic content. Some researchers have observed that many video games are violent in nature and feature death and destruction (Dominick 1984; Loftus and Loftus 1983). One American survey reported that the great majority of video games involved participants in acts of destruction, killing or violence (Bowman and Rotter 1983). More recent observations, however, have revealed a wide range of thematic types, with violent games not invariably dominating the scene. Loftus and Loftus (1983) identified three principal conceptual ingredients of video games:

1.   Sound and fury. 'Flashing lights, bizarre noises and continuously displayed, astronomical scores.'

2.   Death and destruction. Various games involved violence of one sort or another, often taking the form of military weaponry.

3.   Complete control. The example given here was a game called *Pong*. Everything is electronic, with no moving parts as in traditional arcade type video games. *Pong* attained wide social acceptance in the United States. Its price fell rapidly encouraging many household purchases.

Loftus and Loftus then offered what they called a family tree of video games (see Figure 7.1).

Figure 7.1 Family Tree of Video Games

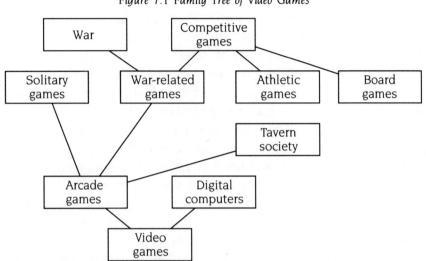

Source: Loftus and Loftus 1983: 6

In the United States, video game arcade managers identified driving-type games (car or motor cycle racing), sports-based games (some with violent themes such as boxing and wrestling, others with non-violent themes such as baseball, basketball, billiards), and others involved puzzle solving. There were a number of different types of game with violent themes. These could be distinguished between ancient adventure games, modern action and Rambo-type games, and games involving combat in outer space (Michaels 1993).

Funk and Buckman (1995) listed six video game categories. *General Entertainment* comprised games in which the main action was a story or game with no fighting or destruction. *Educational* comprised games in which the main theme involved the learning of new information or new ways of using information. *Fantasy Violence* included games in which the action centres on a cartoon character who must fight or destroy things and avoid being killed or destroyed while trying to reach a goal, rescue someone, or escape from something. *Human Violence* covered those games in which the action centres on a human character who must fight or destroy things and avoid being killed or destroyed while trying to reach a goal, rescue someone, or escape from something. *Nonviolent Sports* comprised games in which the action focuses on sports without any fighting or destruction. Finally, *Sports Violence* involved games in which the main action is sport with fighting or destruction. These categories were derived from an initial analysis by the researchers of large range of games available in the marketplace, which was then further corroborated by a survey of views of children and teenagers.

In Britain, Griffiths (1993) provided a longer list of video game types distinguished according to thematic content. Many of the themes identified by Griffiths resemble ones mentioned by other writers. Nine themes were identified in all: (1) *sports simulations* (simulating a variety of different sports); (2) *racers* (simulating motor racing); (3) *adventures* (using fantasy settings and role-playing scenarios with the player assuming the identity of on-screen characters); (4) *puzzlers* (brainteasers which require the player to solve puzzles); (5) *weird games* (a miscellaneous category which do not fit readily under any other heading); (6) *platformers* (games that involve running and jumping along and onto platform, e.g. *Super Mario Brothers*); (7) *platform blasters* (the same as platformers but with a violent theme); (8) *beat 'em ups* (games involving physical violence such as punching and kicking); and (9) *shoot 'em ups* (violent games which involve shooting and various other weapons). It should be noted that three specific 'violent' game types were identified in the above list (i.e. platform blasters, beat 'em ups, and shoot 'em ups), with six, essentially non-violent categories.

Ten game categories were distinguished by *Computer Life* (1995) in a review of more than 80 computer games. Many of these categories resemble the ones outlined by Griffiths (1993). The ten types were called, mythical, homicidal, evergreen, space, arcade, reality, kissing, heroes and villains, wargames, and cynical and rubbish. Mythical, homicidal, space, arcade, heroes and villains and wargames categories were primarily video games containing violence. Some violence-containing games could also be found among the categories called evergreen, reality and cynical and rubbish, although in each of these categories, more non-violent than violence-containing games were listed. Among the cynical and rubbish category, for example, were a number of sports-related games concerning football, cricket and golf. Reality games included mainly flight and car racing simulations. The kissing category comprised a mixture of games involving romantic relationships between on-screen characters, a 'blind date' simulation, and other more voyeuristic games.

What would assist future research into the way children and teenagers react to video games is an even more comprehensive examination of their thematic and production characteristics. So far, research on the impact of video games, whether on cognitive development or social behaviour, has investigated a limited number and range of games and relied upon fairly crude distinctions between games. More taxonomy-related work is therefore needed, combined with the study of players' reactions, which systematically ties in those responses with specific game features or combinations of features. This work has already begun in the context of identifying the features of video games that might usefully be adapted to other human-computer interface designs, particularly those used in constructive learning applications.

Attention also needs to be given to understanding better the nature of children's and teenagers' psychological involvement with different types of computer game. This will become all the more important with the growing trend towards on-line game access. The Internet can provide immediate access to a far greater number and variety of computer games than ever before. Web sites such as LineOne provide games news and reviews, tips about playing, and interactive forums where gamers can talk to each other. In Britain, British Telecom has set up a system called Wireplay that uses a dedicated network server to which players can connect using a standard modem.

Through a systematic and thorough analysis of video game format and content features, and the nature of young players' psychological involvement with different types of electronic game, a picture should emerge of a medium of complexity and diversity offering a variety of potentially constructive applications.

References

Abelson, P. H.
  1982   'The Revolution in Computers and Electronics', *Science* 215: 751-75.

Abbott, M., Palmisano, B., and Dickerson, M.
  1995   'Video Game Playing, Dependency and Delinquency: A Question of Methodology? *Journal of Gambling Studies* 11(3): 287-301.

Adams, E.
  1992   'It's Super Mario to the Rescue', *Los Angeles Times*, September 22, p. E1.

Alperowicz, C.
  1983   'Video games, what's the score?', *React* 12: 10-11.

Anderson, C. A., and Ford, C. M.
  1986   'Affect of the Game Player: Short Term Effects of Highly and Mildly Aggressive Videogames', *Personality and Social Psychology Bulletin* 12: 390-402.

Anderson, C. A., W. E. Dueser, and K. M. DeNeve
  1995   'Hot Temperatures, Hostile Affect, Hostile Cognition, and Arousal: Tests of a General Model of Affective Aggression', *Personality and Social Phychology Bulletin* 21: 434-48.

Anderson, C. A., and Morrow, M.
  1995   'Competitive Aggression Without Interaction: Effects of Competitive Versus Cooperative Instructions on Aggressive Behaviour in Video Games', *Personality and Social Psychology Bulletin* 21: 1020-1030.

Arrindell, D.
  1983   'Math, Science and Technology: Adding it up for Women', *Women and Work* 116: 1-2.

Atari
  1982   *A Public Perspective* (California: Atari)

Athens Banner-Herald
  1984   'Pac Man and Ms Pac Man gobble way to top video spot', *Athens Banner-Herald*, November 11: 21.

Atkinson, R. C., and Wilson, H. A.
  1968   'Computer-assisted Instruction', *Science* 162: 73-77.

Baba, D. M.
  1993   Determinants of Video Game Performance', *Cognitive Issues in Motor Expertise: Advances in Psychology* 102: 57-74.

Baird, W. E., and Silvern, S. B.
  1990   'Electronic Games: Children Controlling the Cognitive Environment', *Early Child Development and Care* 61: 43-49.

Ball, H. G.
  1978   'Telegrams Teach More Than You Think', *Audiovisual Instruction* (May), 24-26.

Baltra, A.
   1990   'Language Learning Through Computer Adventure Games', *Simulation and Gaming* 21(4): 445-452.

Bank Street College Project in Science and Mathematics
   1984   *Voyage of the Mimi* (New York).

Barnes, P.
   1974   'A Study of Personality Characteristics of Selected Computer Programmers and Computer Programmer Trainees' (Unpublished doctoral dissertation, University of Pennsylvania) *Dissertation Abstracts*: 3(3-A), 1440.

Barol, B.
   1989   'Big Fun in a Small Town', *Newsweek* (May 29): 64.

Bell, E. G.
   1955   'Inner-directed and Other-directed Attitudes', in H. A. Witkin, P. K. Oltman, E. Raskin, and S. A. Karp (eds.), A *Manual for the Embedded Figures Test* (Palo Alto, CA: Consulting Psychologists Press, Inc.).

Benedict, J. O.
   1990   'A Course in the Psychology of Video and Educational Games', *Teaching of Psychology* 17(3): 206-208.

Berkeimer Kline Golin/Harris Communications
   1992   *Nintendo of America: Comprehensive Statistics* (Los Angeles, CA)

Billen, A.
   1993   'Could it Be the End for Super Mario? *The Observer* (27 June): 51.

Biocca, F.
   1992   'Communication Within Virtual Reality: Creating a Space for Research', *Journal of Communication* 42: 5-22.

Boden, M. A.
   1977   *Artificial Intelligence and natural Man* (Brighton: Harvester Press).
   1981   *Minds and Mechanisms* (Brighton: Harvester Press).
   1984   'The Meeting of Man and the Machine', in K. P. Jones and H. Taylor (eds.), *The Design of Information Systems for Human Beings* (London: ASLIB).

Bosworth, K.
   1994   'Computer Games and Simulations as Tools to Reach and Engage Adolescents in Health Promotion Activities', *Computers in Human Services* 11(1-2): 109-119.

Bowman, R. F.
   1982   'The 'Pac-Man' Theory of Motivation: Tactical Implication for Classroom Instruction', *Educational Technology* 22: 9, 14-16.

Bowman, R. P., and Rotter, J. C.
   1983   'Computer Games: Friend or Foe', *Elementary School Guidance and Counselling* 18: 25-34.

Bracey, G. W.
   1982   'Computers in Education: What the Research Shows', *Electronic Learning* (November/December): 11-15.

Brand, S.
   1987   *The Media Lab* (New York: Viking Books).

Brandt, R., N. Gross, and P. Coy
    1994   'Sega! It's Blasting Beyond Games and Racing to Build a High-tech Entertainment Empire', *Business Week* (February 2): M66-74.

Brassington, R.
    1990   'Nintendinitis', *New England Journal of Medicine* 322: 1473-74.

Braun, C. M., G. Goupil, J. Giroux, and Y. Chagnon
    1986   'Adolescents and Microcomputers: Sex Differences, Proxemics, Task and Stimulus Variables', *Journal of Psychology* 120: 529-42.

Breakwell, G. M., C. Fife-Shaw, T. Lee, and J. Spencer
    1986   'Attitudes to New Technology in Relation to Social Beliefs and Group Memberships: A Preliminary Investigation', *Current Psychological Research and Reviews* 5: 34-47.

Bright, D. A., and D. C. Bringhurst
    1992   'Nintendo elbow', *Western Journal of Medicine* 156: 667-68.

Brod, C.
    1984   *Technostress: The Human Cost of the Computer Revolution* (Reading, MA: Addison-Wesley).

Bronfenbrenner, U.
    1961   'Some Familial Antecedents of Responsibility and Leadership in Adolescents', in L. Petrullo and B. M. Bass (eds.), *Leadership and Interpersonal Behaviour* (New York: Holt, Rinehart and Winston).

Brooks, B. D.
    1983   (Untitled) in S. S. Baughman and P. D. Ungett (eds.), *Video Games and Human Development: A Research Agenda for the 80s* (Papers and proceedings of the symposium held at the Harvard Graduate School of Education, Cambridge, MA: Gutman Library, Harvard Graduate School of Education).

Brown, R. M., N. L. Brown, and K. Reid
    1992   'Evidence for a Player's Position Advantage in a Video Game', *Perceptual and Motor Skills* 74(2): 547-54.

Brown, R. M., N. L. Brown, D. Delong, and K. Reid
    1995   'Stimulus-response Compatibility and Videogame Performance', *Perceptual and Motor Skills* 80(2): 691-98.

Bruner, J. S.
    1965   'The Growth of Mind', *American Psychologist* 20: 1007-1017.
    1966   'On Cognitive Growth', in J. S. Bruner, R. R. Olver, and P. M. Greenfield *et al.* (eds.), *Studies on Cognitive Growth* (New York: Wiley): 1-67.

Buckman, D. D., and J. B. Funk
    1996   'Video and Computer Games in the 90s: Children's Time Commitment and Game Preference', *Children Today* 24(1): 12-15, 31.

Burbules, N. C., and P. Reese
    1984   *Teaching Logic to Children: An Exploratory Study of 'Rocky's Boots'* (Berkeley: University of California, Lawrence Hall of Science).

Burton, R. R., and J. S. Brown
    1979   'An Investigation of Computer Coaching for Informal Learning Activities', *International Journal of Man-Machine Studies*: 11, 5-24.

Buss, A. H., and A. Durkee
  1957   'An Inventory for Assessing Different Kinds of Hostility', *Journal of Consulting Psychology* 21: 343-49.

Bybee, C., J. P. Robinson, and J. Turow
  1985   'The Effects of Television on Children: What the Experts Believe', *Communication Research Reports* 2: 149-54.

Cahill, J. M.
  1994   'Health Works: Interactive AIDS Education Video Games', *Computers in Human Services* 11(1-2): 159-76.

Calvert, S. L., and S-L. Tan
  1994   'Impact of Virtual Reality on Young Adults' Physiological Arousal and Aggressive Thoughts: Interaction Versus Observation. Special Issue: Effects of Interactive Entertainment Technologies on Development', *Journal of Applied Developmental Psychology* 15(1): 125-39.

Carroll, J. M.
  1982   'The Adventure of Getting to Know a Computer', IEEE *Computer* 15(11): 49-58.

Carroll, J. M., and R. L. Mack
  1984   'Learning to Use a Word Processor: By Doing, by Thinking, and by Knowing', in J. C. Thomas and M. L. Schneider (eds.), *Human Factors in Computer Systems* (Norwood, NJ: Ablex): 13-51.

Carroll, J. M., and J. C. Thomas
  1988   'Fun', SIGCHI *Bulletin* 19(3): 21-24.

Carter, R. C., R. S. Kennedy, and A. C. Bittner
  1980   *Selection of Performance Evaluation Tests for Environmental Research* (Paper presented at the 24th Annual Meeting of the Human Factors Society, San Diego, CA).

Casanova, J., and J. Casanova
  1991   'Nintendinitis', *Journal of Hand Surgery* 16: 181.

Chaffin, J. D.
  1983   *Motivational Features of Video Arcade Games* (Paper presented at the Harvard Graduate School of Education Symposium on Video Games and Human Development, Cambridge, MA, May).

Chaffin, J. D., B. Maxwell, and B. Thompson
  1982   'ARC-ED Curriculum: The Application of Video Game Formats to Educational Software', *Exceptional Children* 49: 173-78.

Chambers, J. H., and F. R. Ascione
  1987   'The Effects of Prosocial and Aggressive Video Games on Children's Donating and Helping', *Journal of Genetic Psychology* 148: 499-505.

Char, C.
  1983   'Research and Design Issues Concerning the Development of Educational Software for Children', in *Chameleon in the Classroom: Developing Roles for Computers* (Symposium presented at the annual meeting of the American Educational Research Association, Montreal).

Clarke, D., and D. Shoech
  1994   'A Computer-assisted Therapeutic Game for Adolescents: Initial Development and Comments', *Computers in Human Services* 11(1-2): 121-40.

Colwell, J., C. Grady, and S. Rhaiti
   1995   'Computer Games, Self-esteem, and Gratification of Needs in Adolescents',
          Journal of Community and Applied Social Psychology 5: 195-206.
Compaine, B. M.
   1983   'The New Literacy', *Daedelus* 112: 129-142.
Computer Life
   1995   *The Insider's Guide to Games* (London: Computer Life, Ziff-Davis UK Ltd).
Condry, J.
   1989   *The Psychology of Television* (Hillsdale, NJ: Lawrence Erlbaum Associates).
Condry, J., and D. Keith
   1983   'Educational and Recreational Use of Computer Technology: Computer In-
          struction and Video Games', *Youth and Society* 15: 87-112.
Cooper, J., and D. Mackie
   1986   'Video Games and Aggression in Children', *Journal of Social Psychology* 16: 726-44.
Corkery, J. C.
   1990   'Nintendo Power', *American Journal of Diseases in Children* 144: 959.
Corno, L., and E. B. Mandinach
   1983   'The Role of Cognitive Engagement in Classroom Learning and Motivation',
          Educational Psychologst 18: 88-108.
Craig, E. M.
   1987   *Expert and Novice Problem Solving in a Complex Computer Game* (Unpublished doc-
          toral dissertation, University of California).
Crawford, C.
   1986   *Balance of Power* (Redmond, CA: Microsoft Press).
Creasey, G. L., and B. J. Myers
   1986   Video Games and Children: Effects in Leisure Activities, Schoolwork and Peer
          Involvement', *Merrill-Palmer Quarterly* 32: 251-62.
Creasey, G. L., and S. Vanden Avond
   1992   'The Influence of Home Video Games Upon Children's Social Behaviour and
          Family Life: Results from Two Prospective Studies', in S. Epstein (Chair),
          Nintendo: Aspects of Social Behaviour and Psychology of Video Game Play (Symposium
          conducted at the 22nd annual convention of the Popular Culture Association,
          Louisville, KY, March).
Cross, E. M.
   1972   'The Behaviour Styles, Work Preferences and Values of an Occupational Group:
          Computer Programmers' (Unpublished PhD), *Dissertation Abstracts International*
          32(7-B): 4273-4274.
Curtis, P.
   1992   'Mudding: Social Phenomena in Text-based Virtual Realities', *Intertek* 3(3):
          26-34.
Dalquist, N. R., J. F. Mellinger, and D. W. Klass
   1983   'Hazards of Video Games in Patients with Light-sensitive Epilepsy', *Journal of
          the American Medical Association* 249: 776-77.
Danko, W. D., and J. M. MacLachlan
   1983   'Research to Accelerate the Diffusion of a New Invention: The Use of Personal
          Computers', *Journal of Advertising Research* 23(3): 39-43.

Day, T.
1996   'Fighting Ninetendo Zaps Ailing Polly', *Financial Mail on Sunday* (August 11): 3.

Deutsch, M.
1993   'Educating for a Peaceful World', *American Psychologist* 48: 510-17.

Dickerson, M., and J. Gentry
1983   Characteristics of Adopters and Non-adopters of Home Computers', *Journal of Consumer Research* 10: 225-34.

Dominick, J. R.
1984   'Video Games, Television Violence and Aggression in Teenagers', *Journal of Communication* 34: 136-47.

Donald, M.
1993   Human Cognitive Evolution: What We Were, What We Are Becoming', *Social Research* 60: 143-70.

Donchin, E.
1983   'Video Games and Learning', Paper presented at the Symposium on ''Video-games and Human Development: A Research Agenda for the 80's'' (Harvard University, Cambridge, MA, May 22-24).
1995   'Video Games as Research Tools: The Space Fortress Game', *Behaviour Research Methods, Instruments and Computers* 2292: 217-23.

Donnerstein, E., R. Slaby, and L. Eron
1994   'The Mass Media and Youth Violence', in J. Murray, E. Rubinstein, and G. Comstock (eds.), *Violence and Youth: Psychology's Response* (Washington DC: American Psychological Association), II.

Doob, A. N., and Wood, L. E.
1972   'Catharsis and Aggression: Effects of Annoyance and Retaliation on Aggressive Behaviour', *Journal of Personality and Social Psychology* 22: 156-62.

Doolittle, J. H.
1995   'Using Riddles and Interactive Computer Games to Teach Problem-solving Skills', *Teaching of Psychology* 22(1): 33-36.

Dorval, M., and M. Pepin
1986   'Effect of Playing a Video Game on Measure of Spatial Visualisation', *Perceptual and Motor Skills* 62: 159-62.

Dugdale, S., and D. Kibbey
1982   *Green Globs and Graphing Equations* (Computer programme; Pleasantville, NY: Sunburst Communications).

Dweck, C. S., W. Davidson, S. Nelson, and B. Enna
1978   'Sex Differences in Learned Helplessness. II. The Contingencies of Evaluative Feedback in the Classroom', *Developmental Psychology* 14: 268-76.
—   'Sex Differences in Learned Helplessness. III. An Experimental Analysis', *Developmental Psychology* 14: 277-78.

Eagly, A. H.
1987   'Reporting Sex Differences', *American Psychologist* 42(7): 755-56.

Edinger, J. A., and M. L. Patterson
1983   'Nonverbal Involvement and Social Control', *Psychological Bulletin* 93: 30-56.

Eggers, J. R., and J. F. Wedman
  1984   'The Growing Obsolescence of Computers in Education', *Educational Technology*
          7: 27-29.

Egli, E. A., and L. S. Meyers
  1984   'The Role of Video Game Playing in Adolescent Life: Is There a Reason to Be
          Concerned?', *Bulletin of the Psychonomic Society* 22: 309-12.

Eisele, J. E.
  1981   'Computers in the Schools: Now That We Have Them ...?', *Educational Technology*
          21: 10, 24-27.

Eisenstadt, G.
  1993   'That's Where the Money Is', *Forbes* 151(2) (18 January): 56-57.

Ellis, D.
  1984   'Video Arcades: Youth and Trouble', *Youth and Society* 16: 47-65.

Equal Opportunities Commission
  1983   *Information Technology in Schools: Guidelines of Good Practice for Teachers of* I. T. (London:
          Borough of Croydon).

Escobedo, T. H.
  1992   'Play in a New Medium: Children's Talk and Graphics at Computers', *Play and
          Culture* (2): 120-40.

Evra, J. van
  1990   *Television and Child Development* (Hillsdale, NJ: Lawrence Erlbaum Associates).

Eysenck, H. J., and S. B. G. Eysenck
  1975   *Manual for the Eysenck Personality Questionnaire* (London: Routledge and Kegan
          Paul).

Favaro, P. J.
  1982   'Games for Cooperation and Growth—An Alternative for Designers', *Softside* 6:
          18-21.

Favelle, G. K.
  1994   'Therapeutic Applications of Commercially Available Computer Software', *Computers in Human Services* 11(1-2): 151-58.

Fennema, E.
  1981   'Attribution Theory and Achievement in Mathematics', in S. R. Yussen (ed.),
          The Development of Reflection (New York: Academic Press): 124-42.

Ferguson, D. A.
  1987   '"RSI": Putting the Epidemic to Rest', *Medical Journal of Australia* 117: 213-214.

Feshbach, S., and J. Singer
  1971   *Television and Aggression* (San Francisco, CA: Jossey-Bass).

Fisher, S.
  1994   'Identifying Video Game Addiction in Children and Adolescents', *Addictive Behaviours* 19(5): 545-53.

Fling, S., L. Smith, T. Rodriguez, D. Thornton, E. Atkins, and K. Nixon
  1992   'Video Games, Aggression, and Self-esteem: A Survey', *Social Behaviour and
          Personality* 20(1): 39-45.

Forrest, P.
  1984   'Hello High School, Bye Bye Micro', *Primary Teaching and Micros* (September):
          6-9

Forsyth, A. S, Jr.
1986 'A Computer Adventure Game and Place Location Learning: Effects of Map Type and Player Gender' (Unpublished doctoral dissertation, Utah State University, Logan).

Forsyth, A. S., and D. F. Lancy
1987 'Simulated Travel and Place Location Learning in a Computer Adventure Game', *Journal of Educational Computing Research* 3: 377-94.

Fredrickson, J., B. Warren, H. Gillott, and P. Weaver
1982 'The Name of the Game is Literacy', *Classroom Computer News* (May/June): 23-27.

Freud, A.
1928 *Introduction to the Technique of Child Analysis* (trans. L. P. Clark; New York: Nervous and Mental Disease Publishing).

Friedland, R. P., and J. N. St. John
1984 'Video-game Palsy: Distal Ulnar Neuropathy in a Video Game Enthusiast', *New England Journal of Medicine* 311: 58-59.

Friedman, T.
1995 'Making Sense of Software: Computer Games and iNteractive Textuality', in S. G. Jones (ed.), *Cybersociety: Computer-Mediated Communication and Community* (Thousand Oaks, CA: Sage).

Friedrich-Cofer, L., and A. H. Huston
1986 'Television Violence and Aggression: The Debate Continues', *Psychological Bulletin* 100: 364-71.

Friedrich, O.
1983 'The Computer Moves In', *Time* 121(1): 14-24.

Frude, N.
1983 *The Intimate Machine: Close Encounters with New Computers* (London: Century Publishing).

Fuller, M., and H. Jenkins
1995 'Nintendo® and New World Travel Writing: A Dialogue', in S. G. Jones (ed.), *Cybersociety: Computer-Mediated Communication and Community* (Thousand Oaks, CA: Sage): 57-72.

Funk, J. B.
1992 'Video Games: Benign or Malignant?', *Journal of Developmental and Behavioural Pediatrics* 13(1): 53-54.
1993a 'Reevaluating the Impact of Video Games', *Clinical Paediatrics* 32(2): 86-90.
1993b 'Video Games', *Adolescent Medicine: State of the Art Reviews* 4: 589-98.
1995 'Video Violence Might Provoke Real-life Tragedy', *American Academy of Pediatric News*: 16-21.

Funk, J. B., and D. D. Buckman
1995 'Video Game Controversies', *Pediatric Annals* 24: 91-94.
1996 Playing Violent Video and Computer Games and Adolescent Self-concept', *Journal of Communication* 46(2): 19-32.

Gabel, D.
1983 'What's in a Game?', *Personal Computing* (April): 63-69.

Gagnon, D.
1985 'Video Games and Spatial Skills: An Exploratory Study', *Educational Communication and Technology Journal* 33: 263-75.

Gallup, G.
  1982   'The Typical American Teenager, *Seattle Times* (May 19): 17.

Gardner, J. E.
  1991   'Can the Mario Bros. Help? Nintendo Games as an Adjunct in Psychotherapy
          with Children', *Psychotherapy* 28: 667-670.
  1993   'Nintendo Games', in C. E. Schaefer and D. Cangelosi (eds.), *Play Therapy
          Techniques* (Jason Arondon, Inc.: Northvale, NJ): 273-80 (Repr. from *Psychotherapy:
          Theory, Research and Practice* 28 [1991]: 667-70.)

Gastaut, H., H. Regis, and F. Bostem
  1962   Attacks Provoked by Television and Their Mechanism', *Epilepsia* 3: 438-45.

Gauntlett, D.
  1995   *Moving Experiences: Understanding Television's Influences and Effects* (London: John
          Libbey).

Gauvain, M.
  1993   'The Development of Spatial Thinking in Everyday Activity', *Developmental Review*
          13: 92-121.

Gershuny, J.
  1978   *After Industrial Society* (London: Macmillan).
  1983   *Social Innovation and the Division of Labour* (Oxford: Oxford University Press).

Getman, G. N.
  1983   'Computers in the Classroom: Bane or Boom?', *Academic Therapy* 18(5): 517-521.

Gibb, G. D., Bailey, J. R., Lambirth, T. T., and Wilson, W. P.
  1983   'Personality Differences in High and Low Electronic Video Game Users', *Journal
          of Psychology* 114: 159-65.

Ginzberg, E.
  1982   'The Mechanization of Work', *Scientific American* 247: 3, 66-76.

Gomez, L. M., D. E. Egan, and C. Bowers
  1986   'Learning to Use a Text Editor: Some Learner Characteristics That Predict
          Success', *Human-Computer Interaction* 2: 1-23.

Gopher, D., M. Well, and T. Bareket
  1994   'Transfer of Skill from a Computer Game Trainer to Flight', *Human Factors* 36(3):
          387-405.

Graybill, D. J. R. Kirsch, and E. D. Esselman
  1985   'Effects of Playing Violent Versus Non-violent Video Games on the Aggressive
          Ideation of Children', *Child Study Journal* 15: 199-205.

Graybill, D., M. Strawnink, T. Hunter, and M. O'Leary
  1987   'Effects of Playing Versus Observing Violent Versus Non-violent Video Games
          on Children's Aggression', *Psychology: Quarterly Journal of Human Behaviour* 24:
          1-7.

Greenburg, J.
  1981   'Games Addicts Play', *Forbes*: 102.

Greenfield, P. M.
  1983   'Video Games and Cognitive Skills', in S. S. Baughman and P. D. Claggett
          (eds.), *Video Games and Human Development: A Research Agenda for the 80s* (Cam-
          bridge, MA: Harvard Graduate School of Education): 19-24.

1984   *Media and the Mind of the Child: From Print to Television, Video Games and Computers* (Cambridge, MA: Harvard University Press).

1990   'Video Screens: Are They Changing How Children Learn?', *Harvard Education Letter* 6(2): 1-4.

1993   'Representation Competence in Shared Symbol Systems: Electronic Media From Radio to Video Games', in R. R. Cocking and K. A. Renniger (eds.), *The Development and Meaning of Psychological Distance* (Hillsdale, NJ: Lawrence Erlbaum Associates): 161-83.

1994   'Video Games as Cultural Artifacts', *Journal of Applied Developmental Psychology* 15(1): 3-12.

Greenfield, P. M., G. Brannon, and D. Lohr

1994   'Two-dimensional Representation of Movement Through Three-dimensional Space: The Role of Video Game Expertise', *Journal of Applied Developmental Psychology* 1(1): 87-103.

Greenfield, P. M., and C. P. Childs

1991   'Developmental Continuity in Biocultural Context', in R. Cohen and A. W. Siegel (eds.), *Context and Development* (Hillsdale, NJ: Lawrence Erlbaum Associates): 135-59.

Greenfield, P. M., and J. Lave

1982   'Cognitive Aspects of Informal Education', in D. Wagner and H. Stevenson (eds.), *Cultural Perspectives on Child Development* (San Francisco, CA: Freeman): 181-207.

Greenfield, P. M., L. Camaioni, P. Ercoloni, L. Weiss, B. A. Lauber, and P. Perrucchini

1994   'Cognitive Socialization by Computer Games in Two Cultures: Inductive Discovery or Mastery of an Iconic Code', *Journal of Applied Developmental Psychology* 15(1): 59-85.

Greenfield, P. M., P. de Winstanley, H. Kilpatrick, and D. Kaye

1994   'Action Video Games and Informal Education: Effects on Strategies for Dividing Visual Attention', *Journal of Applied Developmental Psychology* 15(1): 105-23.

Greer, D, P. Potts, J. C. Wright, and A. C. Huston

1982   'The Effects of Television Commercial Form and Commercial Placement on Children's Social Behaviour and Attention', *Child Development* 53: 611-19.

Griffiths, M.

1996   *Video Games and Children's Behaviour* (Psychology Division, Nottingham Trent University).

Griffiths, M. D.

1989   *The Cognitive Activity of Fruit Machine Players* (Paper presented at the Cognitive Psychology Section Conference, British Psychological Society, Cambridge, September).

1990   'The Acquisition, Development and Maintenance of Fruit Machine Gambling in Adolescence', *Journal of Gambling Studies* 6: 193-204.

1991a   'The Observational Analysis of Adolescent Gambling in UK Amusement Arcades', *Journal of Community and Applied Social Psychology* 1: 309-20.

1991b   'Amusement Machine Playing in Childhood and Adolescence: A Comparative Analysis of Video Games and Fruit Machines', *Journal of Adolescence* 14: 53-73.

1993   'Are Computer Games Bad for Children?', *The Psychologist: Bulletin of the British Psychological Society* 6: 401-407.

1995   *Adolescent Gambling* (London: Routledge).

1996   *Video Games and Children's Behaviour* (Paper presented at Electronic Media, Interactive Technology and Children Conference, Cheltenham and Gloucester College of Higher education, Cheltenham, June 21-22).

Griffiths, M. D., and I. Dancaster
1995   'The Effect of Type A Personality on Physiological Arousal While Playing Computer Games', *Addictive Behaviours* 20: 543-48.

Griffiths, M. D., and C. Hilton
1994   *Computer Game Playing in Adolescence* (Paper presented at the British Psychological Society (Social Psychology Section) Conference, Oxford, September).

Griffiths, M. D., and N. Hunt
1993   'The Acquisition, Development and Maintenance of Computer Game Playing in Adolescence' (Paper presented at the British Psychological Society, London Conference, City University, December).

1995   'Computer Game Playing in Adolescence: Prevalence and Demographic Indicators', *Journal of Community and Applied Social Psychology* 5: 189-93.

Guberman, S. R., and P. M. Greenfield
1991   'Learning and Transfer in Everyday Cognition', *Cognitive Development* 6: 233-60.

Guiliano, V. E.
1982   'The Mechanization of Office Work', *Scientific American* 247: 3, 148-66.

Gunter, B.
1985   *Dimensions of Television Violence* (Aldershot, UK: Gower).

Gutman, D.
1982   'Video Games Wars', *Video Game Player* (fall) (Whole issue).

Haddon, L.
1992   'Explaining ICT Consumption: The Case of the Home Computer', in R. Silverstone and E. Hirsch (eds.), *Consuming Technologies: Media and Information in Domestic Spaces* (London: Routledge): 82-96.

Hall, P. H., Nightingdale, J. J., and MacAulay, T. G.
1985   'A survey of Microcomputer Ownership and Usage', *Prometheus* 3(1): 156-73.

Hansard
1981   *Control of Space Invaders and Other Electronic Games* (6th Series, Vol. 5, May 18-June 5; London: HMSO).

Harris, S.
1994   *Media Influences on Cognitive Development* (Unpublished manuscript, 1992, cited in Greenfield *et al.* 1994).

Hart, E. J.
1990   'Nintendo Epilepsy', *New England Journal of Medicine* 322: 1473.

Harter, S.
1986   'Processes Underlying the Construction, Maintenance, and Enhancement of the Self-concept in Children', in J. Suls and A. G. Greenwald (eds.), *Psychological Perspectives on the Self* (Hillsdale, NJ: Lawrence Erlbaum Associates): 141-63.

1987   The Determinants and Mediational Role of Global Self-worth in Children', in N. Eisenberg (ed.), *Contemporary Topics in Developmental Psychology* (New York: Wiley): 219-42.

Hayes, B., D. F. Lancy, and B. Evans
  1985   'Computer Adventure Games and the Development of Information-processing Skills', in G. H. McNick (ed.), *Comprehension, Computers, and Communication* (Athens, GA: University of Georgia Press): 60-66.

Hess, R. O., and I. T. Miura
  1985   'Gender Differences in Enrolment in Computer Camps and Classes', *Sex Roles* 13: 193-204.

Horn, E., H. A. Jones, and C. Hamlett
  1991   'An Investigation of the Feasibility of a Video Game System for Developing Scanning and Selection Skills', *Journal of the Association for Persons with Severe Handicaps* 16(2): 108-15.

Hubbard, P.
  1991   'Evaluating Computer Games for Language Learning', *Simulation and Gaming* 22: 220-23.

Huff, G., and F. Collinson
  1987   'Young Offenders, Gambling and Video Game Playing', *British Journal of Criminology* 27: 401-10.

Humphries, F.
  1993   'Nintendo's Not Playing Around', *Asian Business* 29(1): 64.

Hunter, J.
  1994   'Authoring Literacy: From Index to Hypermedia', *Canadian Journal of Communication* 19: 41-52.

IPAT
  1979   *Administrator's Manual for the 16PF* (Champaign, IL: Institute for Personality and Ability Testing).

Irwin, A. R., and A. M. Gross
  1995   'Cognitive Tempo, Violent Video Games, and Aggressive Behaviour in Young Boys, *Journal of Family Violence* 10: 337-50.

ITC
  1996   *Television: The Public's View* (London: Independent Television Commission).

Johnstone, B.
  1993   'True Believers', *Far Eastern Economic Review* 155(51): 71-72.

Johnstone, B., and M. Howell
  1991   'Technology in Japan: Multimedia Mania', *Far Eastern Economic Review* 154(51): 37-41.

Jones, M. B.
  1984   'Video Games as Psychological Tests', *Simulation and Games* 15: 131-57.

Jones, M. B., W. P. Dunlap, and I. Bilodeau
  1986   'Comparison of Video Game and Conventional Test Performance', *Simulation and Games* 17: 435-46.

Jones, M. B., R. S. Kennedy, and A. C. Bittner Jr.
  1981   'A Video Game for Performance Testing', *American Journal of Psychology* 94: 143-52.

Kafai, Y. B.
  1995   *Minds in Play: Computer Game Design as a Context for Children's Learning* (Hillsdale, NJ: Lawrence Erlbaum Associates).

Kaplan, S. and S. Kaplan
　1981　'A Research Note: Video Games, Sex and Sex Differences', *Social Science* 56: 208-212.

Kawashima, T. *et al.*
　1991　'Development of Skill of Children in the Performance of the Family Computer Game "Super Mario Brothers"', *Journal of Human Ergology* 20(2): 199-215.

Keepers, G. A.
　1990　'Pathological Preoccupation with Video Games', *Journal of the American Academy of Child and Adolescent Psychiatry* 29: 49-50.

Kelly, A. E., and J. B. O'Kelly
　1994　'Extending a Tradition: Teacher Designed Computer-based Games', *Journal of Computing in Childhood Education* 5(2): 153-66.

Kennedy, R. S., A. C. Bittner, Jr., and M. B. Jones
　1981　'Video-game and Conventional Tracking', *Perceptual and Motor Skills* 53: 310.

Kestenbaum, G. I., and L. Weinstein
　1985　'Personality, Psychopathology and Developmental Issues in Male Adolescent Video Game Use', *Journal of the American Academy of Child Psychiatry* 24: 329-333.

Keys, W., and M. N. B. Ormerod
　1976　'A Comparison of the Pattern of Science Subject Choices for Boys and Girls in the Light of Pupils' Own Expressed Subject Preferences', *School Science Review* 58: 343-50.

Kiddoo, T.
　1982　'Pacman meets GI Joe?', *Soldiers* 37(9): 20-23.

Kiesler, S., J. Seigel, and T. W. McGuire
　1984　'Social Psychological Aspects of Computer-mediated Communications', *American Psychologist* 39: 1123-34.

Kiesler, S., and L. Sproull
　1986　'Reducing Social Context Cues: Electronic Mail in Organizational Communication', *Management Science* 32(11): 1492-1512.

Kiesler, S., L. Sproull, and J. S. Eccles
　1983　'Second Class Citizens', *Psychology Today* 17(3): 41-48.
　1985　'Pool Halls, Chips, and War Games: Women in the Culture of Computing', *Psychology of Women Quarterly* 9: 451-62.

Kinder, M.
　1991　*Playing with Power in Movies, Television and Video Games: From Muppet Babies to Teenage Mutant Ninja Turtles* (Berkeley, CA: University of California Press).

Kirsch, D., and P. Maglio
　1994　'On Distinguishing Epistemic from Pragmatic Action', *Cognitive Science* 18(4): 513-49.

Klein, M. H.
　1932　*The Psychoanalysis of Children* (London: Hogarth).
　1984　'The Bite of Pac-man', *Journal of Psychohistory* 11: 395-401.

Kokush, R.
　1994　'Experiences Using a PC in Play Therapy With Children', *Computers in Human Services* 11(1-2): 141-50.

Kolko, D. J., and P. M. E. Rockard-Figueroa
1985 'Effects of Video Games on the Adverse Corollaries of Chemotherapy in Pae-diatric Oncology Patients', *Journal of Consulting and Clinical Psychology* 53: 223-28.

Koop, E.
1982 'Surgeon General Sees Danger in Video Games', *New York Times* (November 10): A-16.

Korich, M., and H. Waddell
1986 A *Comparative Study of Age and Gender Influecnes on Television Taste* (Unpublished manuscript; Univesity of California, LA).

Krichevets, A. N., E. B. Sirotkima, I. V. Yevsevicheva, and L. M. Zeldin
1995 'Computer Games as a Means of Movement Rehabilitation', *Disability and Rehabilitation: An International Multidisciplinary Journal* 17(2): 100-105.

Kubey, R., and R. Larson
1990 'The Use and Experience of the New Video Media Among Children and Ado-lescents', *Communication Research* 17: 107-130.

Kuhlman, J. S., and P. A. Bectel
1991 'Video Game Experience: A Possible Explanation for Differences in Anticipation of Coincidence', *Perceptual and Motor Skills* 7(2): 483-88.

Kulik, J. A.
1982 *Interesting Findings from Different Levels of Instruction* (Presented at the annual meeting of the American Educational Research Association, Los Angeles, April).

Kunkel, D., B. J. Wilson, J. Potter, D. Linz, E. Donnerstein, S. L. Smith, E. Blumenthal, and T. Gray
1996 *Content Analysis of Entertainment Television: Implications for Public Policy* (Paper presented at the Duke Conference on Media Violence and Public Policy in the Media, Duke, North Carolina, June 27-29).

Lancy, D. F.
1987 'Will Video Games Alter the Relationship Between Play and Development?', in G. A. Fine (ed.), *Meaningful Play, Playful Meanings* (Champaign, IL: Human Kinetics): 219-30.

Lancy, D. F., H. Cohen, B. Evans, N. Levine, and M. L. Nevin
1985 'Using the Joystick as a Tool to Promote Intellectual Growth and Social Inter-action', *Laboratory for the Comparative Study of Human Cognition Newsletter* 7: 119-25.

Lancy, D. F., and B. L. Hayes
1988 'Interactive Fiction and the Reluctant Reader', *The English Journal* 77: 42-46.

Laurel, B.
1993 *Computers as Theatre* (New York: Addison-Wesley).

Leccese, D.
1989 'Video Games Go Back to the Future', *Playthings* (June): 32-33, 85-88.

Leerhsen, C., M. Zabarsky, and D. McDonald
1983 'Video Games Zap Harvard, *Newsweek* 101: 92.

Leont'ev, A. N.
1981 'The Problem of Activity in Psychology', in J. V. Wertsch (ed.), *The Concept of Activity in Soviet Psychology* (Armink, NY: Sharpe): 37-71.

Lepper, M. R.
   1982   *Microcomputers in Education: Motivational and Social Issues* (Paper presented at the American Psychological Association, Washington, DC, August).

Levin, J. A.
   1981   'Estimation Techniques for Arithmetic: Everyday Math and Mathematics Instruction', *Educational Studies in Mathematics* 12: 421-434.

Levin, J. A., and Y. Kareev
   1981   *Personal Computers and Education: The Challenge to Schools* (Unpublished manuscript, University of California at San Diego).

Levy, S.
   1984   *Hackers: Heroes of the Computer Revolution* (New York: Anchor Press/Doubleday).

Lightdale, J. R., and D. A. Prentice
   1994   'Rethinking Sex Differences in Aggression: Aggressive Behaviour in the Absence of Social Roles', *Personality and Social Psychology Bulletin* 20: 34-44.

Linn, S., and M. R. Lepper
   1987   'Correlates of Children's Usage of Videogames and Computers', *Journal of Applied Social Psychology* 17: 72-93.

Linn, M. C., and A. C. Peterson
   1985   'Emergence and Characterization of Sex Differences in Spatial Ability: A Meta-Analysis', *Child Development* 56: 1479-98.

Lintern, G., and R. S. Kennedy
   1984   'Video Games as a Covariate for Carrier Landing Research', *Perceptual and Motor Skills* 58: 167-72.

Littleton, K., P. Light, R. Joiner, D. Messer *et al.*
   1992   'Pairing and Gender Effects on Children's Computer-based Learning', *European Journal of Psychology of Education* (4): 311-24.

Lockheed, M. E., A. Nielson, and M. K. Stone
   1983   *Some Determinants of Microcomputer Literacy in High School Students* (Paper presented at American Educational Research Association, Montreal, April).

Loftus, G. A., and E. F. Loftus
   1983   *Mind at Play: The Psychology of Video Games* (New York: Basic Books).

Lohman, D. F.
   1979   *Spatial Ability: A Review and Reanalysis of the Correlational Literature* (Tech. Rep. No. 8; Palo Alto, CA: Stanford University Aptitude Research project).

Long, M.
   1983   'True Confessions of a Pac Man Junkie', *Family Weekly* (January 2): 6-10.

Lowery, B. R., and F. G. Knirk
   1982-83   'Micro-computer Video Games and Spatial Visualization Acquisition', *Journal of Educational Technology Systems* 11: 155-66.

Lynch, P.
   1994   'Type A Behaviour, Hostility, and Cardiovascular Function at Rest After Playing Video Games in Teenagers', *Psychosomatic Medicine* 56: 152.

Lynch, W. J.
   1981   *TV Games as Therapeutic Interventions* (Paper presented at the American Psychological Association, Los Angeles, August).
   1983   *Cognitive Retraining Using Microcomputer Games and Commercially Available Software*

(Paper presented at the Meeting of the International Neuropsychological Society, Mexico City, February).

McCorduck, P.
1979   *Machines Who Think* (San Francisco, CA: W. H. Freeman and Company).

McClure, R. F., and F. G. Mears
1984   'Video Game Players: Personality Characteristics and Demographic Variables', *Psychological Reports* 55: 271-76.
1986   'Video Game Playing and Psychopathology', *Psychological Reports* 59: 59-62.

McClurg, P. A., and C. Chaille
1987   'Computer Games: Environments for Developing Spatial Cognition?', *Journal of Educational Computing Research* 3: 95-111.

McCowan, T. C.
1981   'Space Invaders Wrist', *New England Journal of Medicine* 304: 1368.

McIlwraith, R.
1990   *Theories of Television Addiction* (Paper presented at the American Psychological Association, Boston, August).

McKee, V.
1992   'Out of Sight—and Out of Mind? Life and Times', *The Times* (22 September): 5.

McNamee, S.
1995   *Youth, Gender and Video Games: Power and Control in the Home* (Paper presented at the Youth 2000 Conference, Hull, July).

Maccoby, E. E., and C. N. Jacklin
1974   *The Psychology of Sex Differences* (Stanford, CA: Stanford University Press).

Machin, D.
1984   'Mud, Mud glorious Mud', *Telelink* (May): 46.

Mandel, H.
1983   'Dr Video: NCTV Takes Stand on Video Games Violence', *Video Games* (February): 97-98.

Malone, T. W.
1980   *What Makes Things Fun to Learn? A Study of Intrinsically Motivating Computer Games. Technical Report* CIS-7 (Palo Alto: Xerox PARC).
1981a   'Toward a Theory of Intrinsically Motivating Instruction', *Cognitive Science* 4: 333-369.
1981b   'What Makes Computer Games Fun?', *Byte* 6(12): 258-277.

Malone, T. W., and M. R. Lepper
1987   'Making Learning Fun: A Taxonomy of Intrinsic Motivations for Learning', in R. E. Snow and M. J. Farr (eds.), *Aptitude, Learning and Instruction*. III. *Cognitive and Affective Process Analysis* (Hillsdale, NJ: Lawrence Erlbaum Associates).

Mandinach, E. D., and L. Corrio
1985   'Cognitive Engagement Variations Among Students of Different Ability Level and Sex in a Computer Problem Solving Game', *Sex Roles* 13: 241-51

Martin, J., and A. R. D. Norman
1970   *The Computerized Society* (London: Penguin).

Matthews, J., and J. Jessel
1993   'Very Young Children Use Electronic Paint: A Study of the Beginnings of

156   *The Effects of Video Games on Children*

Drawing with Traditional Media and Computer Paintbox', *Visual Arts Research* 19(1): 47-62.

Mayfield, M.
1982   'Video Games Only Fit for Old', USA *Today* (November 10): 1.

Mehrabian, A., and Wixen, W. J.
1986   'Preference for Individual Video Games as a Function of their Emotional Effects on Players', *Journal of Applied Social Psychology* 16: 3-15.

Melancon, J. G., and B. Thompson
1985   'Selected Correlates of Computer Arcade Game Play', *Perceptual and Motor Skills* 61: 1123-29.

Mendelsohn, L.
1983   'U.S. Prepare to Combat the Electronic Sweatshop Image', *Computing* (21 July): 17.

Michaels, J. W.
1993   'Patterns of Video Game Play in Parlours as a Function of Endogenous and Exogenous Factors', *Youth and Society* 25(2): 272-289.

Mick, D., M. Konneman, R. O'Farrell, and J. Isaacs
1983   *Algebra Arcade* (Computer program; Fairfield, CT: Queue).

Miller, D. L. G.
1991   'Nintendo Neck', *Canadian Medical Association Journal* 145: 1202.

Miller, G. G., and D. E. Kapel
1985   'Can Non-verbal Puzzle-type Microcomputer Software Affect Spatial Discrimination and Sequential Thinking Skills of 7th and 8th Graders?', *Education* 106: 160-67.

Miller, S.
1996   'Cable Channel Offers Sonic the Hedgehog Video Game Round the Clock', *The Guardian* (20 June): 4.

Milloy, C.
1991   'Video Wars: The Next Generation', *Washington Post* (January 20): D3.

Mitchell, E.
1983   'The Dynamics of Family Interaction Around Home Video Games', *Personal Computers and the Family* 8: 121-135.

Mitchell, W. G., J. M. Charez, S. Baker, and B. C. Guzman
1990   'Reaction Time, Impulsivity, and Attention in Hyperactive Children and Controls: A Video Game Technique', *Journal of Child Neurology* 5(3): 195-204.

Morley, D.
1994   'Between the Public and the Private: The Domestic Uses of Information and Communication Technologies', in J. Cruz and J. Lewis (eds.), *Viewing, Reading, Listening* (Boulder, CO: Westview): 101-24.

Morlock, H., T. Yando, and K. Nigolean
1985   'Motivation of Video Game Players', *Psychological Reports* 57: 247-50.

Murdock, G., P. Hartmann, and P. Gray
1992   'Contextualizing Home Computing: Resources and Practice', in R. Silvertsone and E. Hirsch (eds.), *Consuming Technologies: Media and Information in Domestic Spaces* (London: Routledge): 146-60.

Murray, J., and S. Feshbach
  1978   'Let's Not Throw Out the Baby with the Bathwater: The Catharsis Hypothesis Revisited', *Journal of Personality* 46: 462-73.

Myers, D.
  1984   'The Patterns of Player-game Relationships: A Study of Computer Game Players', *Simulation and Games* 15: 159-85.
  1990   'A Q-study of Game Player Aesthetics', *Simulation and Gaming* 21(4): 375-396.
  1991   'Computer Game Semiotics', *Play and Culture* 4: 334-46.

Nairman, A.
  1982   'Women, Technophobia and Computers', *Classroom Computer News* 293: 23-24.

Naveteur, J., and J-C. Ray
  1990   'Electrodermal Activity of Low and High Trait Anxiety Subjects During a Frustration Video Game', *Journal of Psychophysiology* 4(3): 221-27.

Nawrocki, L. H., and J. L. Winner
  1983   'Video Games: Instructional Potential and Classification', *Journal of Computer Based Instruction* 10: 80-82.

Neal, L.
  1990   'Implications of Computer Games for System Design', in D. Diaper *et al.* (eds.), *Proceedings of* INTERACT '90 (North Holland: Elsevier): 93-99.

Negroponte, N.
  1993   'HDTV: What's Wrong With This Picture?', *Wired* 1(1): 112.

Nelson, T. M., and D. R. Carlson
  1985   'Determining Factors in Choice Arcade Games and Their Consequences upon Young Male Players', *Journal of Applied Social Psychology* 15: 124-39.

Neustatter, A.
  1991   'Keyboard Junkies', *The Independent on Sunday Review* (November 17): 64.

Newell, K. M., M. J. Carlton, A. T. Fisher, and B. G. Rutter
  1989   'Whole-part Training Strategies for Learning the Response Dynamics of Microprocessor Driven Simulators', *Acta Psychologica* 71: 197-216.

Newsweek
  1981   'Invasion of the Video Creatures', *Newsweek* (November 16): 90-94.

Nicholson, J.
  1984   *Video Games-Threat or Challenge? A Preliminary Report* (Unpublished, University of London).

Oakley, C.
  1994   'SMACK: A Computer Driven Game for At-risk Teens', *Computers in Human Services* 11(1-2): 97-99.

Okagaki, L., and P. A. Frensch
  1994   'Effects of Video Game Playing on Measures of Spatial Performance: Gender Effects in Late Adolescence', *Journal of Applied Developmental Psychology* 15(1): 33-58.

Oltman, P. K., E. Raskin, H. A. Witkin, and S. A. Karp
  1971   GEFT: *Adaptation of the Individually Administered Embedded Figures Test* (Palo Alto: CA: Consulting Psychologists Press Inc.).

Orlofsky, S.
  1982   'Surgeon General Blasts Video Games', *Facts on File* 42: 879.

Oyen, A. S., and J. M. Bebko
    1996   'The Effects of Computer Games and Lesson Contexts on Children's Mnemonic Strategies', *Journal of Experimental Child Psychology* 62(2): 173-189.

Palmer, S.
    1996   *Video Games: A Preliminary Study of Video Game Use by Children Aged Between 8-12 on the Island of St Helena and in Gloucestershire* (Paper presented at the Electronic Media, Interactive Technology and Children Conference, Cheltenham and Gloucester College of Higher Education, Cheltenham, June 21-22).

Parsons, K.
    1995   *Educational Places or Terminal Cases: Young People and the Attraction of Computer Games* (Paper presented at the British Sociological Association Annual Conference, University of Leicester, April).

Papert, S.
    1972   'Teaching Children Thinking', *Program Learning and Educational Technology* 9: 245-255.
    1980   *Mindstorms* (New York: Basic Books).

Pateman, J.
    1981   'Communicating with Computer Programs', *Language and Communication* 1: 3-12.

Patkin, T. T.
    1994   *The Question of Violence in the Construction of Virtual Environments* (Paper presented at the International Conference on Violence in the Media, New York, NY, October).

Pavlik, J.
    1996   *New Media and the Information Superhighway* (Boston, MA: Allyn and Bacon).

Pellegrino, J. W., E. B. Hunt, R. Abate, and S. Farr
    1987   A Computer-based Test Battery for the Assessment of Static and Dynamic Spatial Reasoning Abilities', *Behaviour Research Methods* 19: 231-236.

Pellegrino, J. W., and R. Kail
    1982   'Process Analyses of Spatial Aptitude', in R. J. Sternberg (ed.), *Advances in the Psychology of Human Intelligence* (Hillsdale, NJ: Lawrence Erlbaum Associates), I: 311-65.

Pepin, M., and M. Dorval
    1986   *Effect of Playing a Video Game on Adults' and Adolescents' Spatial Visualisation* (Paper presented at the annual meeting of the American Educational Research Association, San Francisco, CA., April).

Perry, T., C. Truxal, and D. Wallach
    1982   'Video Games: The Electronic Big Bang', *IPEE Spectrum* 19: 20-33.

Pezaris, E., and M. B. Casey
    1991   'Girls who Use "Masculine" Problem-solving Strategies on a Spatial Task: Proposed Genetic and Environmental Factors', *Brain and Cognition* 17: 1-22.

Phillips, C. A., S. Rolls, A. Rouse, and M. Griffiths
    1995   'Home Video Game Playing in Schoolchildren: A Study of Incidence and Patterns of Play', *Journal of Adolescence* 18: 687-691.

Phillips, W. R.
    1991   'Video Game Therapy', *New England Journal of Medicine* 325: 1056-1057.

Piestrup, A. M.
1982 Young Children Use Computer Graphics (Portola Valley, CA: Learning Company).
Playthings
1989 'Playthings Retail Survey of Best-selling Toys', Playthings (May 5): 22.
Professional Association of Teachers
1994 The Street of the Pied Piper: A Survey of Teachers' Perceptions of the Effects on Children of the New Entertainment Technology (Derby, UK)
Provenzo, E. F. Jr.
1991 Video Kids: Making Sense of Nintendo (Cambridge, MA: Harvard University Press).
Quinn, C. N.
1991 'Computers for Cognitive Research: A Hyper Card Adventure Game', 20th Annual Meeting of the Society for Computers in Psychology, 1990, New Orleans, Louisiana) Behaviour Research Methods, Instruments and Computers 23(2): 237-46.
Quittner, J.
1994 'Johnny Manhattan Meets the Furrymuckers', Wired (March): 92.
Rabbit, P., N. Banerji, and A. Szymanski
1989 'Space Fortress as an IQ Test? Predictions of Learning and of Practised Performance in a Complex Interactive Video Game', Acta Psychologica 71: 243-57
Real, M. R.
1996 Exploring Media Culture: A Guide. (Thousand Oaks, CA: Sage).
Redd, W. H., P. B. Jacobsen, M. Dietrill, H. Dermatis, M. McEvoy, and J. C. Holland
1987 'Cognitive-attentional Distraction in the Control of Conditioned Nausea in Paediatric Cancer Patients Receiving Chemotherapy', Journal of Consulting and Clinical Psychology 55: 391-95.
Reid, E.
1995 'Virtual Worlds: Culture and Imagination', in S. G. Jones (ed.), Cybersociety: Computer-mediated Communication and Community (Thousand Oaks, CA: Sage): 164-83.
Reinstein, L.
1983 'de Quervain's Stenosing Tenosynovitis in a Video Games Player', Archives of Physical and Medical Rehabilitation 64: 434-35.
Resnick, H.
1994 'Electronic Technology and Rehabilitation: A Computerized Simulation Game for Youthful Offenders', Computers in Human Services 111-2: 61-67.
Rheingold, H.
1993 The Virtual Community: Homesteading on the Electronic Frontier (New York: Simon and Schuster).
Rice, R. E., and G. Love
1987 'Electronic Emotion: Socio-emotional Content in a Computer-mediated Communication Network', Communication Research 1491: 85-108.
Rieber, L. P.
1996 'Seriously Considering Play: Designing Interactive Learning Environments Based on the Blending of Microworlds, Simulations And Games', Educational Technology Research and Development 44(2): 43-58.

Rivers, R.
  1990	'The Role of Games and Cognitive Models in the Understanding of Complex
	Dynamic Systems', in D. Diaper et al. (eds.), Proceedings of INTERACT '90 (North
	Holland: Elsevier): 87-92.
Roberts, J. M., and B. Sutton-Smith
  1962	'Child Training and Game Involvement', Ethnology 1: 166-85.
Roberts, R. J., Jr., D. Brown, S. Wiebke, and M. M. Haith
  1989	Developmental Differences in Learning a New Skill: The Role of Self-imposed Constraints
	(Paper presented at the biennial meeting of the Society of Research in Child
	Development, Kansas City, MO, April).
Roberts, R. J., Jr. et al.
  1991	'A Computer-automated Laboratory for Studying Complex Perception-action
	Skills', Behaviour Research Methods, Instruments and Computers 23: 493-504.
Roberts, R. J., Jr., and M. Ondrejko
  1995	'Perception, Action, and Skill: Looking Ahead to Meet the Present', in M.M.
	Haith, J. B. Benson, R. J. Roberts, Jr., and B. F. Pennington (eds.), The Development
	of Future-Oriented Processes (Chicago: University of Chicago Press): 138-52.
Robinett, W.
  1982	Rocky's Boots (Portola Valley, CA: Learning Company).
Rogers, C. R.
  1982	'Nuclear War: A Personal Response', APA Monitor 13: 6.
Rogers, E., and J. K. Larsen
  1984	Silicon Valley Fever: Growth of High-Technology Culture (New York: Basic Books).
Rogers, E. M., M. E. Vale, and R. Sood
  1984	Diffusion of Video Games among Teenagers in Silicon Valley (Paper presented at the
	34th Annual Conference of the International Communication Association, San
	Francisco, CA).
Rogoff, B., and J. Lave (eds.)
  1984	Everyday Cognition: Its Development in Social Context (Cambridge, MA: Harvard
	University Press)
Rogoff, J. C., and T. Carlton
  1994	Computer Games in 12-13 Year Olds' Activities and Social Networks (Paper presented
	at the British Psychological Society Annual Conference, April).
Ross, D. H., D. H. Finestone, and G. K. Lavin
  1982	'Letter', Journal of American Medical Association 248: 1177.
Rothery, B.
  1971	The Myth of the Computer (London: Business Books Ltd).
Rushbrook, S.
  1986	'"Messages" of Videogames: Social implications', Dissertation Abstract International
	47: 6.
Rushton, B.
  1981	'Space Invader Epilepsy', The Lancet 1: 501.
Rutkowska, J. C., and T. Carlton
  1994	Computer Games in 12-13 Year Olds' Activities and Social Networks (Paper presented
	at the British Psychological Society Annual Conference, April).

Salas, T.
1990   'Video Game Market Continues to Shine', *Playthings* (January): 38.

Salend, S., and D. Santora
1985   'Employing Access to the Computer as a Reinforcer for Secondary Students', *Behavioural Disorders* (November) 11(1): 30-34.

Salomon, G.
1979   *Interaction of Media, Cognition, and Learning* (San Francisco: Jossey-Bass).

Sanders, J. S.
1984   'The Computer: Male, Female or Androgynous?', *The Computing Teacher* (April): 31-34.

Santrock, J. W.
1970   'Influence of Onset and Type of Paternal Absence on the First Four Eriksonian Development Crises', *Developmental Psychology* 3: 273-74.

Saunders, F. E.
1975   'Sex Roles and the School', *Prospects, Quarterly Review of Education* 5: 362-71.

Schie, E. G. M. van, and O. Wiegman
1996   *Children and Video Games: Relations with Aggressive and Prosocial Behaviour, Social Integration, School Performance and Intelligence* (Paper presented at the Electronic Media, Interactive technology and Children Conference, Cheltenham and Gloucester College of Higher Education, Cheltenham, June): 21-22.

Schiebe, K. E., and M. Erwin
1979   'The Computer as Altar', *Journal of Social Psychology* 108: 103-109.

Schink, J. C.
1991   'Nintendo Enuresis', *American Journal of Diseases in Children* 145: 1094.

Schutte, N. S., J. M. Malouff, J. C. Post-Gordon, and A. L. Rodasta
1988   'Effects of Playing Video Games on Children's Aggressive and Other Behaviours', *Journal of Applied Social Psychology* 18: 454-60.

Scott, D.
1995   'The Effect of Video·Games on Feelings of Aggression', *Journal of Psychology* 129(2): 121-32.

Scribner, S
1986   'Thinking in Action: Some Characteristics of Practical Thought', in R. J. Sternberg and R. K. Wagner (eds.), *Practical Intelligence: Nature and Origin of Competence in the Everyday World* (Cambridge: Cambridge University Press): 13-20.

Secunda, V.
1983   'Pac Man is (a) Gobbling or (b) Nourishing our Kids', *TV Guide* (February 19): 11-12.

Seidel, R. J., A. E. Anderson, and B. Hunter (eds.)
1982   *Computer Literacy* (New York: Academic Press).

Selnow, G. W.
1984   'Playing Video Games: The Electronic Friend', *Journal of Communication* 34: 148-56.

Shaffer, R. A.
1993   'Playing Games', *Forbes* (August 16): 108.

Shallis, M.
   1984   *The Silicon Idol: The Micro Revolution and Its Social Implications* (Oxford: Oxford University Press).

Sheff, D.
   1993   *Game Over: How Nintendo Zapped an American Industry, Captured Your Dollars, and Enslaved Your Children* (New York: Random House).

Sherer, M.
   1994   'The Effect of Computerized Simulation Games on the Moral Development of Youth in Distress', *Computers in Human Services* 11(1-2): 81-95.

Shimai, S., K. Masuda, and Y. Kishimoto
   1990   'Influences of TV Games on Physical and Psychological Development of Japanese Kindergarten Children', *Perceptual and Motor Skills* 70: 771-76.

Shimai, S., F. Yamada, K. Masudu, and M. Tada
   1993   'TV Game Play and Obesity in Japanese School Children', *Perceptual and Motor Skills* 76(3, Pt. 2): 1121-22.

Shotton, M.
   1989   *Computer Addiction?: A Study of Computer Dependency* (London: Taylor and Francis).

Siegal, I. M.
   1991   'Nintendonitis', *Orthopaedics* 14: 745.

Sigel, I. E., and R. R. Cocking
   1977   'Cognition and Communication: A Dialectic Paradigm for Development', in M. Lewis & L. A. Rosenblum (eds.), *Interaction, Conversation, and the Development of Language: The Origins of Behaviour* (New York: Academic Press), V: 207-26.

Silvern, S. B.
   1986   'Classroom Use of Video Games', *Education Research Quarterly* 10: 10-16.

Silvern, S. B., and P. A. Williamson
   1987   'The Effects of Video Game Play on Young Children's Aggression, Fantasy, and Prosocial Behaviour', *Journal of Applied Developmental Psychology* 8: 453-62.

Silvern, S. B., P. A. Williamson, and T. A. Countermine
   1983   *Video Game Playing and Aggression in Young Children* (Paper presented at the Annual Meeting of the Educational Research Association, Montreal, Canada, April).

Simons, G.
   1985   *Silicon Shock: The Menace of the Computer Invasion* (Oxford: Basil Blackwell).

Simpson, B.
   1983   'Why Kids Live Chips', *The Guardian* (December 15): 6.

Small, D., and S. Small
   1982   'The Experts' Guide to Beating *Asteroids, Battelzone, Galazian Ripoff* and *Space Invaders*', *Creative Computing* 18(1): 18-33.

Smith, C. L., and J. M. Stander
   1981   'Human Interaction with Computer Simulation: Sex Roles and Group Size', *Simulation and Games* 12: 345-60.

Sneed, C., and M. A. Runco
   1992   'The Beliefs Adults and Children Hold About Television and Video Games', *Journal of Psychology* 126(3): 273-84.

Soper, W. B., and M. J. Miller
1983   'Junk Time Junkies: An Emerging Addiction Among Students', *School Counsellor* 31: 40-43.

Spelke, E., P. Zelazo, J. Kagan, and M. Hotelchach
1973   'Father Interaction and Separation Protest', *Developmental Psychology* 9: 83-90.

Spence, J.
1988   'The Use of Computer Arcade Games in Behaviour Management', *Maladjustment and Therapeutic Education* 6: 64-68.

Spence, S. A.
1993   'Nintendo Hallucinations: A New Phenomenological Entity', *Irish Journal of Psychological Medicine* 10: 98-99.

Sprandel, G.
1982   'A Call to Action—psychological Impacts of Computer Usage', *Computers and Society* (USA) 12.2: 12-13.

Stefansson, B. *et al.*
1977   'Television Epilepsy and Pattern Sensitivity', *British Medical Journal* 2: 88-90.

Stein, A. H., and L. K. Friedrich
1972   'Television Content and Young Children's Behaviour', in J. P. Murray, E. A. Rubinstein and G. A. Comstock (eds.), *Television and Social Behaviour*. II, *Television and Social Learning* (Washington, DC: U.S. Government Printing Office): 202-317.

Stein, J. S., and M. Linn
1985   'Capitalizing on Computer-based Interactive Feedback: An Investigation of Rocky's Boots', in M. Chen and W. Paisley (eds.), *Children and Microcomputers: Research on the Newest Medium* (Beverly Hills, CA: Sage): 213-27.

Stein, W., and W. Kochman
1984   'Effects of Computer Games on Children's Cooperative Behaviour', *Journal of Research and Development in Education* 18: 1.

Steiner, R.
1996   'Boom Looming in Computer Games Market', *The Sunday Times* (Business Section) (24 November): 9.

Steuer, F. B., J. M. Applefield, and R. Smith
1971   'Televised Aggression and the Interpersonal Aggression of Preschool Children', *Journal of Experimental Child Psychology* 11: 442-47.

Stevens, D. J.
1980   'How Educators Perceive Computers in the Classroom', AEDS *Journal* 13: 221-32.

Stowbridge, M. D., and P. Kugel
1983   'Learning to Learn by Learning to Play', *Creative Computing* (April): 180-88.

Strommen, E. F., S. Razavi, and L. M. Medoff
1992   'This Button Makes you Go Up: Three Year Olds and the Nintendo Controller', *Applied Ergonomics* 23(6): 409-13.

Strover, S.
1984   *Games in the Information Age* (Paper presented at the meeting of the International Communication Association, San Francisco, CA, May).

Subrahmanyan, K., and P. M. Greenfield
1994   'Effect of Video Game Practice on Spatial Skills in Girls and Boys', *Journal of Applied Developmental Psychology* 15(1): 13-32.

Suppes, P.
1966   'The Uses of Computers in Education', *Scientific American* 215: 207-20.

Surrey, D.
1982   'It's Like Good Training for Life', *Natural History* 91: 71-83.

Svebak, S. *et al.*
1992   'Components of Type A Behaviour Pattern as Predictors of Neuroendocrine and Cardiovascular Reactivity in Challenging Tasks', *Personality and Individual Differences* 13(6): 733-44.

Szer, J.
1983   'Video Games as Physiotherapy', *Medical Journal of Australia* 1: 401-402.

Thimbleby, H.
1979   'Computer and Human Consciousness', *Computers and Education* 3: 241-43.

Thomas, P., and R. Macredie
1995   'Games and the Design of Human-computer Interfaces', *Educational Technology Training and Instruction* 31(2): 134-42.

Thornburg, D. D.
1981   'Computers and Society: Some Speculations on the Well-played Game', *Compute!* 14: 12-16.
1982   'Computers and Society', *Compute!* 23: 18.

Tierney, R. J., R. Kieffer, L. Stowell, L. E. Desai, K. Whalin, and A. G. Moss
1992   'Computer Acquisition: A Longitudinal Study of the Influence of High Computer Access on Students' Thinking, Learning and Interaction', *Apple Classrooms of Tomorrow* (Research Rep. No. 16; Cupertino, CA: Apple Computer, Inc.).

Tirre, W. C., and K. K. Raouf
1994   'Gender Differences in Perceptual-motor Performance', *Aviation, Space and Environmental Medicine* 65(5, Sect. 2., Suppl.): A49-A53.

Tjonn, H. H.
1984   'Report of Facial Rashes Among VDU Operators in Norway', in B. G. Pearce (ed.), *Health Hazards of VDTs?* (Chichester: John Wiley).

Toles, T.
1985   'Video Games and American Military Ideology', in V. Mosco and J. Wasko (eds.), *The Critical Communications Review.* 3: *Popular Culture and Media Events* (Norwood, NJ: Ablex): 207-23.

Trachtman, P. A.
1981   'Generation Meets Computers—And They are Friendly. *Smithsonian* 12(6): 50-61.

Trinkaus, J. W.
1983   'Arcade Video Games: An Informal Look', *Psychological Reports* 52: 586.

Tseng-Wen-Sheng
1973   'Psychopathological Study of Obsessive-compulsive Neurosis in Taiwan', *Comprehensive Psychiatry* 14: 139-50.

Tuckman, B. W.
1984   'Thinking out Loud—Why (and Why Not) Teach Computer Usage', *Educational Technology* (February): 35.

Turkle, S.
1984   *The Second Self: Computers and the Human Spirit* (New York: Simon and Schuster).

US *News and World Reports*
1982   'Video Games—Fun or Serious Threat?', US *News and World Report* (February 22): 7.

Vasterling, J. *et al.*
1993   'Cognitive Distraction and Relaxation Training for the Control of Side Effects due to Cancer Chemotherapy', *Journal of Behavioural Medicine* 16: 65-80.

Video Games and Human Development: A Research Agenda for the '80s
1983   (Cambridge, MA: Monroe C Gutman Library)

Waddilove, K.
1984   'The Case for Cost Effective Chalk', *The Guardian* (March 20): 11.

Walker, L. B.
1993   'What's in a Game?', *Washington Post* (November 3): C5.

Ward, R.
1983   'Wasted Potential', *Times Educational Supplement* (November).
1985   'Girls and Computing', *Computer Education* (February 4-5).

Wark, M.
1994   'The Video Game as an Emergent Media Form', *Media Information Australia* (February): 71.

Weinberg, G. M.
1971   *The Psychology of Computer Programming* (New York: Van Nostrand Reinhold).

Weiner, G.
1980   'Sex Differences in Mathematical Performance' in R. Deem (ed.), *Schooling for Women's Work* (London: Routledge and Kegan Paul).

Weizenbaum, J.
1976   *Computer Power and Human Reason* (San Francisco, CA: W. H. Freeman and Company).
1984   *Computer Power and Human Reason* (Harmondsworth, UK: Penguin).

Welch, R. L., A. Huston-Stein, J. C. Wright, and R. Plehal
1979   'Subtle Sex-role Cues in Children's Commercials', *Journal of Communications* 29: 202-209.

Wheelock, J.
1992   'Personal Computers, Gender and an Institutional Model of the Household', in R. Silverstone and E. Hirsch (eds.), *Coonsuming Technologies: Media and Information in Domestic Spaces* (London: Routledge): 97-112.

White, W. B. Jr.
1992   'What Value are Video Games?', USA *Today Magazine* (March): 74.

Wilson, J.
1992   'A Brief History of Gaming: Part 1', *Computer Gaming World* (July).

Winkel, M., D. M. Novak, and H. Hopson
1984   *Personality Factors, Subject Gender, and the Effects of Video Game Content on Aggression in Adolescents* (Paper presented at the annual meeting of the Southwest Psychological Association, Houston, April).
1987   'Personality Factors, Subject Gender, and the Effects of Aggressive Video Games on Aggression in Adolescents', *Journal of Research in Personality* 21: 211-23.

Witkin, H. A. *et al.*
1962   *Psychological Differentiation* (New York: John Wiley).

Wood, D. B.
  1990   'Nintendo's Quest: Staying popular', *Christian Science Monitor* (December 3): 12.
Wood, L. E.
  1980   'An "Intelligent" Program to Teach Logical Thinking Skills', *Behaviour Research Methods and Instrumentation* 12: 256-58.
Zarat, M. M.
  1984   'Cataracts and Visual Display Terminals', in B. G. Pearce (ed.), *Health Hazards of VDTs?* (Chichester: John Wiley).
Zillmann, D.
  1971   'Excitation Transfer in Communication-mediated Aggressive Behaviour', *Journal of Experimental Social Psychology* 7: 153-59.
Zillmann, D., A. H Katcher, and B. Milavsky
  1972   'Excitation Transfer from Physical Exercise to Subsequent Aggressive Behaviour', *Journal of Experimental Psychology* 8: 247-59.
Zimbardo, P.
  1982   'Understanding Psychological Man: A State of the Science Report', *Psychology Today* 16: 15.

INDEX OF MODERN AUTHORS